The Most Needful Thing

A Busy Woman's Guide to Sitting at the Feet of Jesus

AMY S. NEAL

Table of Contents

Week 1

Sitting at the Feet of Jesus

I have to admit that this study was partly inspired by Dr. Seuss. One day as I was picking up my daughter's books for the hundredth time, I picked up Dr. Seuss', "Ten Apples Up On Top", and I thought, I feel like that little creator on the cover trying to balance all those apples. I have all these hats on my head and I am trying my best to balance them all. These days we are so busy with so many things. It seems as if we wear many hats: mother, wife, housekeeper, healer, teacher, provider, etc. As women I believe we often feel stretched and in our efforts to be the perfect woman, we neglect the most needful thing.

In this study we will be seeking God to lead us to a life in which we can do all the things we need to do and still find time to sit at his feet. We will look at 10 roles that women take on (although there may be many more, we will concentrate on 10).

Sometimes we think, oh, I wish things were simple like they used to be. But we will find that women have been busy people since Bible days.

Let's read about this Godly woman in Proverbs 31:10-31.

After reading this scripture look back over it again and list her responsibilities.

_______________________   _______________________

_______________________   _______________________

_______________________   _______________________

_______________________   _______________________

_______________________   _______________________

Whew! Makes me tired just reading about this woman's life. But her payday is in verse 31.

1) The fruit of her hands
2) Praise for her work

Also in verse 28

1) Her children call her blessed
2) Husband calls her blessed
3) They both praise her

Many of us probably feel like this woman in proverbs, many without verses 28 & 31. In the busyness of life, you may not be getting praise from your family. You may actually feel under-valued and unappreciated.

Many of us feel overwhelmed with all of our responsibilities and that takes us to the heart of our study, which is taking off the hats and sitting at the feet of Jesus.

As we go through this study keep in mind that service is good, but worship is better. God's primary purpose for creating us was not service, but rather worship and relationship. We serve out of a worshipful heart, a heart of love toward the object of our affection.

Read Luke 10:38-42

First let's look at the relationship of the people in this passage. Mary and Martha were sisters. They were the sisters of Lazarus, the one Jesus had raised from the dead. This event takes place in the town of Bethany at Martha's house (verse 38). Martha received Jesus in to serve him physically with a good meal. Martha was in the kitchen toiling away. Everything had to be perfect. This was Jesus, the Son of God after all. Mary on the other hand was at Jesus' feet (verse 39). She heard his word; she was interested in what he had to say. A front row seat was not good enough for Mary, she had to get closer, and so she sat at His feet. Sitting at His feet implies humility, not worthy to look at Jesus eye to eye, but instead she bent to her knees and sat at his feet. Sitting at his feet also implies worship and an eagerness to learn, to hear what He has to say.

I think too often we get caught in the same position as Martha, serving instead of sitting. We serve our families, our communities, our church – choir, children's church, Sunday school, special committees, etc. We get so busy serving that we neglect the more needful thing – the sitting at Jesus' feet, hearing Him and worshipping Him. When this happens all of a sudden our service becomes cumbersome as it did with Martha.

Look again at verse 40; the Bible says that Martha was cumbered with <u>much</u> serving. Serving seems to be what Martha did. In the Baptist church we would call her the Head of the Hospitality committee. Any time there was a function that involved food they would call on Martha and she would get the job done. I can imagine Martha as one who would want everything to be just right. The food had to be cooked to perfection. The tables had to be dressed with the finest table clothes and beautiful fresh flowers were probably prepared as centerpieces. She would make sure everything got done and everyone got served. I'm sure she often had the weight of the project on her shoulders because others didn't do their part, can I get an Amen. In so doing the KJV says she became cumbered.

What does it mean to become cumbered?

____

Webster's dictionary defines cumbered as being overloaded, burdened. When I think of this word, I think, "Pack mule" and that's how I feel at times, and I think that must have been how Martha was feeling too.

Have you ever felt cumbered, overloaded, burdened down? If so, take a moment to write down what made you feel that way.

____

Martha began to resent the fact that she was doing all the work and that her sister Mary was not helping. I can imagine that each time she stirred the pot she was becoming hotter and hotter.

Where did Martha go when she got angry and felt resentment toward Mary?

____

The good thing is that this anger and resentment drove her to <u>Jesus</u>. When we're burdened and overloaded is that not the best place to go? As for me, I have found it to be so.

The burdens of the world can weigh us down sometimes, but Jesus says, "Come unto me all ye who labor and are heavy laden and I will give you rest. Take my yoke upon you and learn of me for my yoke is easy and my burden is light." He wants the best for us. Our heavenly Father will not weigh us down, but rather he looses us and frees us to worship and learn of Him. He doesn't say take my yoke and I will make you a slave, but He says take my yoke and learn of Me. Put your neck in the yoke *with* Him and let him lead. That way you won't get a stiff neck, and make your muscles all tired and achy. Just surrender! Easy, right? I think that for many of us that is a very hard thing to do; to release all control and fully trust in Jesus.

Do you find it easy to totally surrender or do you feel like you have to pull the whole load alone?

____

____

So here comes Martha, angry and frustrated, and pours her heart out to Jesus, or it may better be stated, she vents. She asks Jesus, "don't' you care that my sister has left me to serve alone?" She seems to be saying, "Lord, I know that you are just and righteous, does it not seem unfair, unjust even, that I serve alone while my sister sits around doing nothing?" She even goes further to say, "Make her help me." To those who have young children does this not sound familiar? Mommy, Mommy, Johnny's not helping me clean our room. Make him help!

What does Jesus say to her (verse 41 – 42)?

____

____

He lovingly answers her. I can almost see him put his beautiful hand on her shoulder and shake his head from side to side as He says, "Martha, Martha, you are careful and troubled about many things". And it was true; Martha went to the trouble to do many things, not just this supper. But many times Martha was the one serving, the one left alone to get the job done.

Can anybody relate to Martha? I know there are times when I feel like I am Martha. We feel like we have to take care of everything – the kids, our husbands, the house, the laundry, the finances, and on top of all that many of us have jobs outside the home. Remember those hats piled high on our heads? We are careful and troubled about so many things. In many ways we feel like we are the glue that holds everything together when in reality we are not. God is the one who holds it all together and when we try to do something that only He can do, what happens? Exactly, we become cumbered, burdened, and weary. We must be careful that we do not become resentful and bitter. We must guard against it, because even though we have much to do, those things are what brings us purpose, gives us opportunity to follow in our Saviors footsteps by serving others.

Why do you think that Martha was in the kitchen instead of at the Savior's feet? There is no right or wrong answer, just want you to think.

____

____

____

I think the answer can be found in Matthew 4:18-19. Read the scripture and write below why these people became unfruitful.

____

____

____

In this verse the cares of the world had choked out the word and made them unfruitful. Similar to what happened to Martha the care of cooking the meal and making sure everything was just right choked out her being at the feet of Jesus, hearing his word. And so it happens to us. We get so busy with the cares of the world. The things that have to be done that we forget or neglect to sit at the feet of Jesus. And the worse thing of all is that we need to sit with Jesus in order to do those other things well. For at his feet we get instruction on how to fulfill our roles in a way that brings glory and honor to God.

So let's go to the feet of Jesus at this time and seek wisdom to be the women of faith that He would have us to be. That we may wear our hats high and proud and not be burdened down and cumbered by them.

Week 2

Wife

For those who are married what do you think of when you think of the word "wife"? What images does this word evoke?

____

____

____

Answers may be different for those who have been married a short time, still in the honeymoon stage, and those of us who have been married for a while.

When I think of the word wife the first thing I think of is union, being united to someone else. I also think of words such as love, companionship, helper, lover, and friend.

If your first thoughts of the word wife were your responsibilities instead of your relationship it could be that the cares of this world have choked your marriage, maybe even to the point of death. It is true that the word wife evokes images of responsibility such as caregiver and servant but those things should come out of a heart of love. If when we think of our being a wife as being slave to a man, then we **will** become resentful, we **will** feel undervalued, and we **will** become bitter.

Is this what God meant for women, to be the submissive slaves of men? Many people will pull out Ephesians 5:22 and say that is exactly what He meant.

Let's take off the wife hat for a moment and place it at the feet of Jesus and let's ask Him. Stop and pray for guidance, wisdom, and understanding of what God's view of a wife is.

We find Eve, the first wife in Genesis, so let's go back to the beginning. God created them male & female – they were to have dominion over other creators – not that the man would have dominion over the woman. Genesis 2:21 says that the woman was taken from Adam's rib to be a <u>help meet</u>. See in the appendix the Hebrew words and meaning for "help meet".

What is the Hebrew word:

____

What does it mean?

____

Adam called her <u>woman</u> – taken from man.

____

What is the Hebrew word for woman:

____

What does it mean?

____

Notice that neither of these meanings have anything to do with being a slave or a servant to man. We will discuss this further a little later. Genesis 2:24 says, man shall leave mother and father and <u>cleave</u> unto his wife.

What is the Hebrew word for cleave (see appendix):

____

What does it mean?

____

The man is to leave and cleave. There are too many men today that want their wife and their mommy too. God said leave and cleave, to become one flesh with his wife. This is the most intimate relationship one can have. More intimate than that of mother & daughter, mother & son, father & daughter, father & son, sister & brother, etc. There is no earthly relationship more intimate than that of husband and wife.

Read verse 25, "And they were both naked, the man and his wife, and were not ashamed". Now tell me, can you get any more intimate than that? To stand naked in front of someone and not be ashamed; the key word is intimacy. Why is this intimate relationship so important in the scripture?

____

I believe it is because it is symbolic of our relationship with Christ. Even in the Garden of Eden, from the very beginning, God was pointing us to Jesus.

When sin enters is when we have problems. Adam and Eve had it made in Eden until the day that Eve took of the fruit and gave it to Adam and he also ate the fruit.

What happened when they partook of the fruit? (Gen. 3:7)

____

Their eyes were opened and they realized they were naked. So the first thing they did was try to cover up. And when they hear the voice of God, evidently a familiar voice, they tried to hide amongst the trees. I find it interesting this whole exchange between God, Adam, and Eve. First Adam says, I heard you, but I was afraid, because I was naked. And God ask, "Who told thee that thou was naked? It was almost as though God was saying I didn't tell you so how did you know that you were naked? As I read this scripture I couldn't help but think of my two year old. She likes to be naked and finds no shame in it. She would be very content to go anywhere that way. But there will come a day when she will realize that running around naked is not appropriate and she would be ashamed to do so. That is what happened to Adam and Eve. Satan was right that their eyes would be opened, but he did not tell them that their innocence would be lost. He did not tell them that life would no longer be full of joy, excitement, and blessed communion with God, a time when God provided everything for them and came in the cool of the day to have fellowship with them.

Don't you sometimes envy the carefree spirit, the innocence of a child? Not to have any worries, but just to run free, knowing that our God is caring for us and watching out for our well-being. That is what Satan robbed us of in the garden.

Not necessarily related to topic of wife — but interesting I think. Look at verse 9:

And out of the ground made the LORD God to grow every tree that is pleasant to the sight, and good for food; the tree of life also in the midst of the garden, and the tree of knowledge of good and evil.

The tree of life and the tree of knowledge of good and evil in the midst of the garden are two different trees. God distinguished them from the others.

Which tree does God tell Adam not to eat of? See verses 16 & 17:

"16 And the LORD God commanded the man, saying, Of every tree of the garden thou mayest freely eat:

17 But of the tree of the knowledge of good and evil, thou shalt not eat of it: for in the day that thou eatest thereof thou shalt surely die."

He told them not to eat of the tree of the knowledge of good and evil. Why did He not tell Adam not to eat of the tree of life? Was it because God knew our nature? That if he told Adam, he would end up eating of that tree also? Was he being merciful, even way back in the Garden of Eden? Read verses 22 through 24 and decide for yourself:

"22 And the LORD God said, Behold, the man is become as one of us, to know good and evil: and now, lest he put forth his hand, and take also of the tree of life, and eat, and live forever:

23 Therefore the LORD God sent him forth from the garden of Eden, to till the ground from whence he was taken.

24 So he drove out the man; and he placed at the east of the garden of Eden Cherubims, and a flaming sword which turned every way, to keep the way of the tree of life."

If Adam had eaten of the tree of life, we would have to live under the curse for eternity. Thank God, he didn't have that temptation or Eve either.

We see that God killed animals and provided skins for clothing for Adam and Eve. Can you imagine how Adam and Eve must have felt? The Bible does not say it, but I believe that God made Adam and Eve watch while he slays those animals. Remember these animals before the curse were not fierce and vicious as they were after the curse. Adam and Eve knew them more as pets than as ferocious beast. Adam had named each one and I am sure he had grown to love each creature. But here we find one of those creatures, because of Adam and Eve, in the hand of a righteous God being sacrificed. The animal or animals were innocent at this point and yet they died to cover the sin of Adam and Eve. I don't know about you but I am very tender hearted when it comes to seeing an animal hurt. I can hardly watch those Discovery Channel programs that show how animals live in the wild. When they show one animal killing the other it breaks my heart. Consider how Adam and Eve felt when they saw this animal, the one Adam had named, fed, and cared for. When they heard the squalls of the animal as the life was being drained from its body. As they watched it writhe in pain. Can you imagine the impact it had on Adam and Eve? We know that it had impact enough that they knew and had evidently passed along to their children that it took a blood sacrifice to satisfy God for sin. Remember Cain and Abel? Oh don't you see Jesus all through this scripture foreshadowing things to come.

The Woman's Curse

Unto the woman he said, I will greatly multiply thy sorrow and thy conception; in sorrow thou shalt bring forth children; and thy desire *shall be* to thy husband, and he shall rule over thee.

There are 3 components to the woman's curse: 1) pain in childbirth, 2) desire to your husband, and 3) husband rule over you.

Pain in Child Birth

I don't know if Eve had children before and there was no pain in childbirth or if this is when she actually starts having children. We know that even before the fall it was God's plan for humanity to reproduce because in Genesis 1:28 God tells them to "be fruitful and multiply". However because there is no scripture reference to any children before the fall, I believe that they did not have any children before this time. So from this I believe that childbirth was not the punishment for sin but rather the *pain* in childbirth.

Look in the appendix at the Hebrew word for sorrow. Write the Hebrew word and its meaning:

____

Childbirth is one of woman's greatest blessings, but because of the curse this most blessed event is full of pain, literal, excruciating pain. Thanks to medicine we can now get epidurals and relieve this pain during the actual birth, but we still feel the after affects. For several days following the birth we feel the pain and soreness of what has taken place in our bodies.

Desire to Husband

Look in the appendix at the Hebrew word for desire. Write the Hebrew word and its meaning:

____

Desire is an emotion and affection. Women are naturally more emotional and more affectionate than men; God made us this way. Why is it that little girls dream of their Prince Charming, but little boys don't want anything to do with girls until they get about 13? It is because our desire, (our curse) is to our man and early in our lives we start trying to fulfill that desire. Why would desire for our husband be a curse? It seems kind of strange that the thing we love and desire would become our curse. In many marriages especially with individuals who are unequally yoked and where there is abuse, curse may seem like a subtle word for the situation.

Another thought and I believe maybe the most accurate reason that God made our desire be to our husband was to continue that symbolism that I spoke of earlier. Remember the intimate relationship between husband and wife is a reflection of the relationship between Christ and the Church. So as the wife's desire should be to her husband so too should the churches desire be to her groom, Jesus Christ. As a Christian, Jesus is my bridegroom and my desire should be to Him and Him alone. There should be no other god, no other priority above Him. He should be the song of our mouths, the beat of our hearts, the light of our eyes, the desire of our touch, and our all in all. Church, He is our Prince Charming and one day He will come to take us home.

How can this desire become a curse? If we put other things before him — our husbands, our children, our jobs, our busy lives. We are busy women, no doubt, but nothing, absolutely nothing, should hinder us from our desire. And nothing, absolutely nothing should take the place of our desire to our Lord. If we become so busy that we rob God of our time, our talents, ourselves, then we will see our desire become a curse. I believe that no Christian can be truly happy living afar from their Savior. God is saying to us, "I want you!" Don't let anything stand in your way of getting to Him.

And most importantly if we reject him, it will surely become an everlasting curse to us. Anyone who dares trample underfoot the precious blood of Christ will surely perish. They will live under the curse for all eternity. "

Wherefore? Because *they sought it* not by faith, but as it were by the works of the law. For they stumbled at that stumblingstone;

As it is written, Behold, I lay in Sion a stumblingstone and rock of offence: and whosoever believeth on him shall not be ashamed". (Romans 9:32-33)

Husband Rule Over You

We often hear preached that a woman's curse is sorrow in child bearing but our curse is also that we have become subordinate to man, and in many ways, especially in our society, this is probably the greater curse. And remember women, this is a curse and because of sin, it is our curse to bear. I find no way scripturally to get around it. There have been times when I have thought that God loved man more than woman, but the more I study and the more I understand the character of God, I realize that just isn't true.

We see in Numbers 27:1-11 that God allowed women to possess the inheritance of their fathers if they had no sons. Jesus spoke to women as he went about doing good. He even spoke to some women that others did not speak to. The first people to see Jesus after his resurrection were women. Jesus did more for women's lib than any liberal ever did. All the women's libbers and the bra burners ever did was get us double the work we had before. Now not only do we care for our husbands, our children, and our home, but we also go out and work. Thanks a lot. Jesus was no respecter of persons. He respected authority and a line of order, but he never rejected a woman just because she was female. He never looked at a woman as less than a man or even less than an animal as many men of that day did. No wonder the Pharisees sought to kill him. He was turning their philosophy, their prejudices, upside down. Jesus had the audacity to say that we were heirs, even joint heirs with Jesus Christ. 1 Peter 3:7 puts us on equal standing with our husbands in the grace of God, "Likewise, ye husbands, dwell with *them* according to knowledge, giving honor unto the wife, as unto the weaker vessel, and as being heirs together of the grace of life; that your prayers be not hindered.

God's intention originally was for us to be on equal footing with man. I tend to agree with Scoffield who says, "The entrance of sin, which is disorder, makes necessary a headship, and it is vested in man." Not that God loves women less or thinks less of them but disorder had entered the world and this was how He chose to reinstall order, because it was after all the woman that was deceived.

Read Genesis 1:26-27.

God created mankind after his image; He gave them dominion over sea creatures, flying creatures, land creatures, and all creeping things. Notice the Bible says that God gave **them** dominion.

Who does he mean when he says <u>them</u>? (Verse 27)

____

Verse 27 answers this question. It says, ". . . male and female created he <u>them</u>".

So from the beginning God had woman working together in harmony with man – on equal standing. The man having rule over us is the part of the curse that is even greater than the physical pain of childbirth because this curse requires us to submit ourselves. Submission is something very hard to do. It is harder to submit than to fight. It requires our becoming humble, putting someone else above ourselves. This is probably the hardest part of the curse, but it is when we fulfill this role that we are most like our Savior. Are we better than our Savior? He humbled himself to the Father, emptied himself of His glory, came to a world that despised and rejected Him, was beaten and bruised, died on a cruel cross for a world that was unworthy of Him. Is there any humility, any submission, greater than that?

See the scriptures listed in the Appendix to see that God has established an order. Women are to be submitted to their husband, men are to be submitted to Christ, and Christ is to be submitted to God. So we are all called to submission.

What are the images that come to your mind when you hear the word submit?

____

More than likely they are negative images. Webster's Dictionary defines submit as "to yield oneself to the authority or will of another". I believe it is a willing release – not forced – so we still have the power. The question is will we release it – let it go – give it to God?

In Ephesians 5:22 the Bible says "Wives submit yourselves unto your husbands, as unto the Lord". Our submission should not be simply out of obedience to man – but out of obedience to God. When we submit to our husbands it is the same as our submitting to the Lord. Keep in mind that these passages were written to church people. That means that both the man and the woman were Christians – if you are unequally yoked with an unbeliever – this scripture is going to be very hard for you. First of all, your unbelieving husband is not going to be submitted to Christ which is what the next verse calls for, therefore the whole order of things is messed up. In that case the only advice I could give is that you pray for the salvation of your husband. Covenant with others to help you pray for the salvation of your husband. This is an order that is arranged by God and the only way it can work is if we are all in submission and in our place. Consider a group of cheerleaders who are making a pyramid. They need the strong people on the bottom and the smaller people on top. Each person must take their place, their position; otherwise the pyramid will not be complete. Also if one of the bottom or middle cheerleaders decides to withdraw from the pyramid, then the whole thing will collapse. So it is with the order of marriage each person must be in his or her position for it to work.

So to fulfill this role of wife proudly we must do the following: we must surrender fully to God and his plan for our lives. If He created us women and He gave us a desire for a man, then we must submit to that man and in so doing we are submitting to our God. Do not confuse submission to slavery. We are **not** called to be a man's servant, but rather we are to be a help-mate to our husbands. To help someone does not mean that you do it for them, but rather it means that you share in the effort to achieve a common goal. <u>Working together</u>, like two oxen in a yoke. The Bible actually refers to marriage as two people yoked together. In 2 Corinthians 6:14 the Bible warns us not to be unequally yoked together with unbelievers. So if we are yoked together, then we are on equal footing and the person with the reigns should not be the husband or the wife; but rather God should control the reigns. This will never happen if you are unequally yoked with an unbeliever. If the two don't work together then they are just pulling in two different directions. But if one ox submits to the other, then they can go forward in one direction, working together. Not that we're oxen, we're not that smart, remember the bible refers to us as sheep. I believe that often in our day, Christian women become overwhelmed with all their responsibilities. Women try to follow the perfect picture of a wife, the June Cleaver, if you will, but we live in a different day. Most women today work outside of the home, including Christian women, yet they are still trying to bear all of the responsibilities of yesteryear (caring for husband, children, and home) as well as work a full time job. No wonder we become burdened down and overloaded. Women we are in this together with our husbands, if we are helping them bear their curse (providing for the family) then they should also be helping us bear ours. Don't feel like you have to do it all. You can't, and it will become unhealthy to your relationship if you do. So let's work together with our husbands, raising happy, healthy children and serving the Lord.

It is true that we are different than men, thank God, Amen. And we have different roles in God's plan but God does not value us less. He has a plan and a purpose for each of us. To be a wife is truly a blessing from God. My dear friend, if being a wife has become a burden to you, then you need to sit at the feet of Jesus and let Him renew your love and give you a mind to enjoy this wonderful role that he has placed you in.

If you enjoy your role of a wife and take pleasure from your relationship take a moment to thank God. Write down just a simple prayer of thanks.

____

____

____

It may be that some of you are struggling and have lost the joy of being a wife. God loves you and he wants to heal you spiritually. It is no accident that you are going through this study at this time. God is ministering to you. Open your heart to Him.

If you are one who feels the role of a wife to be cumbersome and overbearing, write a simple prayer to God to help renew a joy and an excitement about the role of wife and about your spouse. Then take a moment to sit at His feet and allow Him to respond to you.

____

____

____

Week 3

Mother

Oh what a heavy hat we wear. Mommy, Mommy, Mommy! Kids crying, arguing, fighting, squealing, biting, something going on all the time, this is the role of a mother. It's true a mother's job is never done. There is no one who knows self-sacrifice like the mother of a small child. And if you think the toddler years are rough wait till you get to the teen-age years. You do realize that teen-agers know everything don't you.

When you think of the word mother, what are the first images that come to your mind?

____

____

____

For me when I think mother, the first images that come to my mind are my children and my own mother. I think of my children, oh how I love them, and how thankful I am for them. I think of the huge responsibility of raising a child. I also think of my own mother and how she cared for me. She was my example of a mother. In many ways, the way I raise my children is because that is the way she raised me. We will talk more about a mother being a teacher in week five.

There is no doubt that the role of mother can be very tiring. It can absolutely wear you down. Mothers with small children are worried with changing diapers, feeding and pacifying crying and cranky babies, being playmate, and on and on. It seems that it gets a little easier as they grow older, but then those teen years set in and we're wondering why we ever chose to have children, just kidding, but they can make you pull your hair out. Some of you may have grown children who are causing you worry. They may be into things that are ungodly and harmful to them and because they are grown, you feel that you can't do anything about it. But dear friend you can, take it to Jesus. Between toddler and teen, baseball and ballet, it is easy to let the cares of the world choke out our joy of being a mother. So let's just stop for a minute, take off the mother hat and lay it at the feet of Jesus.

Write a simple prayer asking God to help us learn of Him how to be a better mother and how to have joy in the journey.

____

____

____

I believe that to be a mother is one of the greatest gifts that God has given to the female race. It is intertwined with our curse after the original sin. It is actually in two parts. First, God promises to use the woman to destroy Satan, Genesis 3:15, "And I will put enmity between thee and the woman, and between thy seed and her seed; it shall bruise thy head, and thou shalt bruise his heel." This is the first reference to Christ and it is through a woman that our Savior would come into the world.

Look in the appendix and write the definition for the word enmity.

____

____

Satan had deceived the woman and became her enemy. He used her to bring sin into the world, but God would use the woman to bring salvation into the world.

Secondly, Genesis 3:16 says, "Unto the woman he said, I will greatly multiply thy sorrow and thy conception; in sorrow thou shalt bring forth children; . . . ."

Let's look at the word sorrow taken from these verses once again. From the appendix we find that it means:

____

Not sorrow as in the way that we think of sorrow – to be sad, or to be sorry, but it is describing the pain associated with childbirth. I was not sorrowful or sad during childbirth but until I received my epidural there was great pain and without the benefit of drugs there would have been much more pain.

We find then in verse 20 of Genesis that Adam gives his wife the name Eve because she is the _mother_ of _all living_. So women, never think that God does not place importance on women. Never think or let anyone tell you that a woman is valued less than a man. God entrusted woman with the greatest task this earth has ever seen – "For unto us a child is born, unto us a son is given . . . (Isaiah 9:6) it was by a woman that our Savior entered this world.

This one hat actually encompasses many more hats such as caregiver, provider, psychiatrist, and counselor. We will look at the caregiver and the provider separately later in the study. Right now we will focus on mother as a counselor. A mother probably has more influence on a child than anyone else in the world. As I write about the influence of mothers my mind automatically goes to this familiar poem by William Ross Wallace: "The Hand That Rocks the Cradle":

Blessings on the hand of women!
Angels guard its strength and grace,
In the palace, cottage, hovel,
Oh, no matter where the place;
Would that never storms assailed it,
Rainbows ever gently curled;
For the hand that rocks the cradle
Is the hand that rules the world.
Infancy's the tender fountain,
Power may with beauty flow,
Mother's first to guide the streamlets,
From them souls unresting grow--
Grow on for the good or evil,

Sunshine streamed or evil hurled;

For the hand that rocks the cradle

Is the hand that rules the world.

Woman, how divine your mission

Here upon our natal sod!

Keep, oh, keep the young heart open

Always to the breath of God!

All true trophies of the ages

Are from mother-love impearled;

For the hand that rocks the cradle

Is the hand that rules the world.

Blessings on the hand of women!

Fathers, sons, and daughters cry,

And the sacred song is mingled

With the worship in the sky--

Mingles where no tempest darkens,

Rainbows evermore are hurled;

For the hand that rocks the cradle

Is the hand that rules the world.

Oh the influence we have over our children, oh the awesome responsibility! "Sunshine streamed or evil hurled". Do we set them in the light, do we shine the light on them and inspire them to grow and to be all that God has purposed for them to be or do we stunt their growth and discourage them with our dark evil words?

Time to Reflect

Take just a moment to reflect on how you have influenced your children and pray that God would help you be a mother that inspires.

____

____

____

____

Mother's Influence

Now let us look at some women in the Bible and explore how they influenced their children. First we find Samson who desires a wife of the Philistines in Judges 14:1-3:

"¹ And Samson went down to Timnath, and saw a woman in Timnath of the daughters of the Philistines.

² And he came up, and told his father and his mother, and said, I have seen a woman in Timnath of the daughters of the Philistines: now therefore get her for me to wife.

³ Then his father and his mother said unto him, *Is there* never a woman among the daughters of thy brethren, or among all my people, that thou goest to take a wife of the uncircumcised Philistines?"

In your own words what were Samson's Mother and Father saying to him?

To me they were basically saying, "Don't do it, that girl is not right for you". And they were right. Later in the chapter we find that this marriage only brought Samson heartache and pain.

Next read the verses on Ahaziah from 2 Chronicles 22

"¹ And the inhabitants of Jerusalem made Ahaziah his youngest son king in his stead: for the band of men that came with the Arabians to the camp had slain all the eldest. So Ahaziah the son of Jehoram king of Judah reigned.

² Forty and two years old *was* Ahaziah when he began to reign, and he reigned one year in Jerusalem. His mother's name also *was* Athaliah the daughter of Omri.

³ He also walked in the ways of the house of Ahab: for his mother was his counsellor to do wickedly.

⁴ Wherefore he did evil in the sight of the LORD like the house of Ahab: for they were his counselors after the death of his father to his destruction."

Who was his counselor and how did she counsel him?

His mother was his counselor and she counseled him to do evil.

And lastly let's look at Rebekah and her influence on Jacob. Read Genesis Chapter 27. What did Rebekah influence Jacob to do?

____

____

____

He actually stole his brother, Esau's blessing. "Remember that it was Jewish custom for the Father to give his blessing to the firstborn son. Being the oldest child, even though they were twins, Esau was actually the firstborn so the blessing was to be his. As we find in this Chapter, Rebekah influences Jacob to steal his brother's blessing. That seems cruel, deceitful, and downright dirty if you read it on the surface, but if you go back in scripture you will find that God loved Jacob and hated Esau. God himself had promised the blessing to Isaac. Therefore Rebekah was really only a tool in the hand of God to fulfill his promise and his prophecy. For he said the following in Genesis 25:23

And the LORD said unto her, Two nations *are* in thy womb, and two manner of people shall be separated from thy bowels; and *the one* people shall be stronger than *the other* people; and the elder shall serve the younger.

Who said this to Rebekah?

____

So we should not look at this from our own humanistic perspective and try to understand how a mother could do this to her son. This was one of those what we like to call a "God Thing". It was a prophecy made by God himself and it would be fulfilled. It doesn't actually say in scripture, but Rebekah must have had Godly influence to influence Jacob as she did. You will also find if you read in Chapter 25 that Esau had sold his birthright, which was the right of the blessing, to Jacob for a bowl of pottage. Esau had sworn unto Jacob that he would sell him his birthright, but you don't see Esau explaining this to Isaac in Chapter 27, so don't feel sorry for Esau. He wasn't just some poor guy whose mother hated him and whose brother deceived him; he was a wicked person who did not value the birthright or any other spiritual thing.

Oh the power of influence! And mothers, we have it. We have just seen through some Biblical examples the power of influence. You have probably seen a mother's influence in people that you know and if you are a mother you are probably exercising it with your own children. So knowing that we wield so great a power, let us be cautious how we use it. May we always seek God's face and His guidance, may He influence us, and we in turn influence them.

Mother's Love

Probably the greatest love outside of the Love of God is a mother's love. For most mothers there is practically nothing that could separate them from the love for their child. As I think of a mother's love my mind goes to the story in the Bible of Hannah. Remember how she so desired a child from the Lord. This desire was a burning fuel inside of her and anyone who has longed to have a child and not been able to can relate to how Hannah felt. In First Samuel Chapter One Hannah, who had been barren, pleads for a child and the Lord grants her request. Finally she conceives and bares a son. I can just image Hannah as she sits there rocking her baby, kissing him on the forehead, admiring God's handiwork of creation. I can remember when both of my children were babies just sitting for hours and admiring them, and I remember how swollen with love my heart felt for that new little being. But with Hannah her time of nursing and caring for her child was bitter sweet for she had promised to give him back to the Lord. True to her word Hannah takes her son Samuel to serve in the temple and leaves him there. This I can't even imagine. After holding this child in her arms for the months until it was weaned and then having to walk away from it must have been one of the most agonizing and excruciating things that Hannah had ever had to do. Yet her love for God and her holy fear for God left her no other choice. Oh what better Christians we would be if we had that kind of love for God and holy fear of him. The kind that would make us forsake our most natural passions to be true to Him. When we consider Hannah and what she gave up to keep her promise to God it makes our broken promises seem quiet shallow.

Hannah never forgot her son Samuel; her love was ever present with him. Read 1 Samuel 2:19

"Moreover his mother made him a little coat, and brought *it* to him from year to year, when she came up with her husband to offer the yearly sacrifice."

What did Hannah make Samuel when she came to see him?

____

Can you see Hannah through the year as she would gather the materials to make the fabric? Then she would take care to estimate how much she thought he would grow from year to year. She would weave the garment together, each strand with love for her son and praise to her God.

How often did she get to see him?

____

When did she get to see him?

____

God had made this time of offering even more blessed for Hannah. She was allowed to worship her God and to see the precious son that He had given her.

As I consider the subject of mother, I am drawn to this story, I suppose because even though Hannah did not get to keep Samuel and raise him until he was fully grown, yet she did the best thing that a mother can do for their child and that is to give it to Jesus. Many times in our churches we will have dedication services and say that we are dedicating our child to the Lord, but are we really or is that just a ceremony. Would we really be willing to dedicate our child to the Lord's service if it meant we had to give it up as soon as it was weaned? Hard question I know. To give up my child would be like ripping my heart out of me and draining my life's blood, so I'm not sure that I could truly say yes even though I know in my heart that "yes" is the correct answer for a child of God.

Since most of us are not faced with such a demanding dilemma I guess our question is will we dedicate our children in the sense that we will encourage them to be all that God has purposed for them to be. Will we live a life before them that glorifies God and will we influence them to make Godly choices.

Mother – Child's Greatest Advocate

A mother is also a child's greatest advocate. From the definition in the appendix what does the term advocate mean?

____

____

____

So as mothers we naturally defend, support, and promote our children, we plead their cause and we stand in their stead. There ain't nobody goin' get your back like Momma. You can mess with me but don't you dare mess with one of my babies. I will defend my child no matter what. Even if they are wrong I will step in the middle and advocate on their behalf to make things right. I didn't say that I would uphold them in wrongdoing, but I certainly will be there to show them where they were wrong and help them understand how to make things right.

We find a great example in the scripture of a mother being the advocate for her son. Read the following scripture taken from 1 King Chapter 1:

"[15] And Bathsheba went in unto the king into the chamber: and the king was very old; and Abishag the Shunammite ministered unto the king.

[16] And Bathsheba bowed, and did obeisance unto the king. And the king said, What wouldest thou?

[17] And she said unto him, My lord, thou swarest by the LORD thy God unto thine handmaid, *saying*, Assuredly Solomon thy son shall reign after me, and he shall sit upon my throne.

[18] And now, behold, Adonijah reigneth; and now, my lord the king, thou knowest *it* not:

[19] And he hath slain oxen and fat cattle and sheep in abundance, and hath called all the sons of the king, and Abiathar the priest, and Joab the captain of the host: but Solomon thy servant hath he not called.

[20] And thou, my lord, O king, the eyes of all Israel *are* upon thee, that thou shouldest tell them who shall sit on the throne of my lord the king after him.

[21] Otherwise it shall come to pass, when my lord the king shall sleep with his fathers, that I and my son Solomon shall be counted offenders.

²² And, lo, while she yet talked with the king, Nathan the prophet also came in.

²³ And they told the king, saying, Behold Nathan the prophet. And when he was come in before the king, he bowed himself before the king with his face to the ground.

²⁴ And Nathan said, My lord, O king, hast thou said, Adonijah shall reign after me, and he shall sit upon my throne?

²⁵ For he is gone down this day, and hath slain oxen and fat cattle and sheep in abundance, and hath called all the king's sons, and the captains of the host, and Abiathar the priest; and, behold, they eat and drink before him, and say, God save king Adonijah.

²⁶ But me, *even* me thy servant, and Zadok the priest, and Benaiah the son of Jehoiada, and thy servant Solomon, hath he not called.

²⁷ Is this thing done by my lord the king, and thou hast not shewed *it* unto thy servant, who should sit on the throne of my lord the king after him?

²⁸ Then king David answered and said, Call me Bathsheba. And she came into the king's presence, and stood before the king.

²⁹ And the king sware, and said, *As* the LORD liveth, that hath redeemed my soul out of all distress,

³⁰ Even as I sware unto thee by the LORD God of Israel, saying, Assuredly Solomon thy son shall reign after me, and he shall sit upon my throne in my stead; even so will I certainly do this day.

³¹ Then Bathsheba bowed with *her* face to the earth, and did reverence to the king, and said, Let my lord king David live forever."

Who is Bethsheba pleading for?

____

What is she pleading for?

____

It was Solomon who had been promised the throne and Bethsheba, his mother, intended to see that he got it. This was no small thing. This was the person who would rule the nation of Israel.

Mother's Comfort

When you're feeling down there is no one that can comfort you like momma. We have seen that our mother influences us, she is our advocate, and she loves us, so it is no wonder this is the place where we would find comfort. God even compares himself to a mother in Isaiah 66:13

> "As one whom his mother comforteth, so will I comfort you; and ye shall be comforted in Jerusalem."

The term comfort used here actually entails much more than what we think of when we think of comfort. When I look up comfort in the Webster's Dictionary I find a definition that is what I would expect to find:

Comfort: **1:** to give strength and hope to: CHEER **2:** to ease the grief or trouble of: CONSOLE But look at the Hebrew definition of comfort in the appendix.

Write down some of the terms given in this definition.

____

____

This definition includes such words as sorry, repent, regret, pity. The greatest comfort we will ever encounter is the comfort we feel when we repent and are forgiven. That is true comfort. To repent of our sins and know that we are forgiven, it takes away the guilt, it gives us sweet release, and oh what comfort.

So as mothers our comfort comes from our children's knowledge that we will forgive them, we will have pity on them, we will have comfort and compassion for them, just as God has for us. May God always be able to point us out as an example of a comforter.

Mother's Honor

Exodus 20:12 says that we are to honor father & mother, not only that but this is a commandment with promise.

> "Honor thy father and thy mother: that thy days may be long upon the land which the LORD thy God giveth thee."

What does God tell us we should do to our father and mother?

____

This is a commandment that I remind my teenage daughter of quite often. This is a commandment from God. It is not a suggestion. God expects us to honor our parents. But notice that God did not just say – honor thy father. No he included the mother in this commandment. Somewhere down the course of time women somehow lost the honor that God had ascribed them. We know that in many cultures of the bible days women were not thought of as much more than an animal. But God from the beginning of time said that we were worthy of honor. I can't say it enough, "Women, don't lose sight of who you are in the eyes of God. Don't lose sight of your value and your worth in the eyes of our heavenly Father."

Why are we to honor our father and mother according to Exodus 20:12?

____

This is a commandment with promise. Of the Ten Commandments that God gave to Moses on Mount Sinai this is the only one that is followed by a promise. God may have attached this promise because we find under the Levitical law that parents could stone disobedient children. So it would follow that if you did not honor your mother and father your days would not be long upon the earth. But I believe it is way more than just the threat of death, but it is a character-istic that God desires to see in children. We learn about authority first through our parents. They are the first role models that we have. If children can learn to submit to the authority of their parents and honor their parents then submission to the heavenly Father and honor to the heavenly Father would naturally follow suit. Also I believe that honor for our parents is not just for when we are young, but even when we become adults, and our parents are up in age, we should still honor them. Too often we push them to the side as though they don't matter once they become unproductive, but God expects us to honor them always.

So mother you are an honored vessel in the eyes of God. He has chosen to use you to rear children and he expects those children to give you honor because you deserve it. I know that sometimes the everyday demands of being a mother can sometimes absolutely drain you of all your energy physically, emotionally, and spiritually. But remember that in the big picture they are only small once. Try to enjoy every minute because before you know it they are grown and gone on to live their own lives. Cherish them! And remember that God sees you and your work as precious and worthy of honor. Don't ever let anyone including society tell you that being a mother isn't important or that you are giving up your life and your dreams by being a mother. Your job is the most important job in the world. Never forget that you are molding the next generation and the greatest authority of all, our God, has said you are to be honored.

Week 4

Worker/Provider

Over the years the role of a woman has changed in many ways. One way in which our role has changed is in the fact that most women work outside of the home today. For some this is by choice but for most this is necessary in order to provide for the needs of the family. When my mom and dad were young they built their house as they saved money. They would take a little from each check, go to the lumber yard, buy lumber and build what they could. Then the next week they would go get some more supplies and build a little more. They continued to do this until they finally had it complete. And when it was done, it was paid for. I can hardly even imagine living without a mortgage. A mortgage is just part of life for families today. With the cost of materials it would take 30 years to build a house if we did it the way my mom and dad did. So the majority of Americans today do live with a mortgage. We also have the high cost of insurance to contend with as well as the ever increasing cost of gasoline. At this writing gasoline in our area is at $3.54 a gallon. We all have car loans, bank loans, boat loans, Visa, and Mastercard just to name a few. Most Americans today are up to their eye balls in debt. Oh and don't forget Uncle Sam, those dreaded taxes. Therefore it is not feasible for most women to stay at home. It is true that we live the good life, we have all of the nice things in life, but those are just velvet chains. For you see they may be velvet but nevertheless they are chains. We are bound! We cannot just say I don't want to work, because we are bound by our debt. Americans have become like the children of Israel in Egypt. We have become slaves to the almighty dollar and the desire to have things. We don't hear much preached about covetousness but is that not what this huge sin comes down to? Wanting to have what others have? Long gone are the days of June Cleaver, staying at home taking care of the house and raising the children. Look at the following statistics from the 2012 data compiled by the U.S Bureau of Labor Statistics:[1] In families with children under 18, 65.4% of women in married couple families work and 67.1% of women in families maintained by women work. In families with children ages 6-17, 69.5% of women in married families work. In that same category, 72.1% of woman who maintain the family work. In families with children under 6, 60.3% of women in married couple families work and 59.9% of women in families maintained by women work.

As you can see from the data over 50% of all women are in the work force as of 2012 and the percentages are even higher for single women and for women with children.

We are only on the third role of a woman and already we have three full time jobs. This is not the God-given plan for women, for the Bible says that God will not put on us more than we can bear. And indeed it was not God that put this heavy load on us. Remember our in Genesis, women were not to be the providers, but the caregivers. But we have desired to be equal to man and so we have gained his curse as well as bearing our own. We are overworked, underappreciated, frayed, and tattered. There are many days when I wonder how I will fit it all in. For a person who is very near being a perfectionist, it is very frustrating because there is no way to do all of our jobs and do them well. It seems we just have to do the best we can and try to get by. When I feel this way I often go back to Proverbs 31 and read about the godly woman of this scripture. Her life was not easy either, but according to the scripture she never complained or was disgruntled, but she just went along doing her work. Can't you just see her whistling while she spins the thread to make clothes for her family? I believe this woman had come to the place to see the work as unto those that she loved so it became a joy to her. If we could come to the place to just do our work with joy and gladness and not let it drag us down we would probably have more pep in our step, more zest in our quest, and more joy in our journey. Everything does not have to be perfect. Remember most of the things we do here are temporary. Don't get caught up in the temporal but live for the eternal. I have come to learn that as a teacher it does not matter if I cover every little topic in my curriculum, I cannot let that trip me up. But what does matter is the relationships that I make with my students. They probably will not remember most of what I have taught them in computer class, but they **will** remember if I treated them

---

[1] http://www.bls.gov/news.release/archives/famee_04262013.pdf

with kindness. They **will** remember if I was fair in my dealing with them. They **will** remember if I was always grumpy or if I was joyful.

I know that it is hard sometime to go to work and be happy and joyful, there is a lot of stress, so take this time to write a prayer to God that he would help you in your busy life, in all phases of your life, even on your job to project the fruits of the spirit to a lost world.

____

____

____

As I studied the scripture I found it difficult to find references for women that worked outside of the home. Other than the woman of proverbs the only one that I could find was Lydia. She was a business woman, she was in sales. Read Acts 16:13-15.

" [13]And on the sabbath * we went out of the city by a river side, where prayer was wont to be made; and we sat down, and spake unto the women which resorted thither.

[14] And a certain woman named Lydia, a seller of purple, of the city of Thyatira, which worshipped God, heard us: whose heart the Lord opened, that she attended unto the things which were spoken of Paul.

[15] And when she was baptized, and her household, she besought us, saying, If ye have judged me to be faithful to the Lord, come into my house, and abide there. And she constrained us."

What did Lydia sell?

____

From what I have read it is unclear if Lydia sold purple dye or if she sold purple fabric. In the bible days who wore purple?

____

So considering that her cliental was royalty she was probably a **wealthy** business woman. Yet she found time for God. She was a working woman, a busy woman, yet her heart longed for more. You see there is no job that will ever fulfill us, we need our creator, we need **GOD!** He truly is the most needful thing. I believe Matthew Henry had a good word about Lydia when he said, "Though she had a calling to mind, yet she was a worshipper of God, and found time to improve advantages for her soul. The business of our particular callings may be made to consist very well with the business of religion, and therefore it will not excuse us from religious exercises alone, and in our families, or in solemn assemblies, to say, We have shops to look after, and a trade to mind; for have we not also a God to serve and a soul to look after? Religion does not call us from our business in the world, but directs us in it. Everything in its time and place."

So whether we work because we have to or whether we work because we want to we should still find time for worship. Many women fall into the boat that I am in, I have to work although I have a young child and a teen age child and my heart desires to be home for them. Others work because they want to, their jobs are their lives. They find their identity in their work. Those in this boat need to take caution that they do not let their jobs become their God. Remember that **anything** that we put before God becomes an idol and is sin.

Rejoice in simplicity and sincerity of life. Read 2 Corinthians 1:12:

"For our rejoicing is this, the testimony of our conscience, that in simplicity and godly sincerity, not with fleshly wisdom, but by the grace of God, we have had our conversation in the world, and more abundantly to you-ward."

Week 5

Teacher

Women who have children also wear the hat of teacher. We are the greatest teachers that our children will ever have. What they learn at home and especially from their mothers are the things that will stick with them throughout their lives. They will normally follow in our footsteps as far as how they live, how they think, and how they act. I teach high school and I may have some influence on my students but I don't have a tenth of the influence on my students as I have on my own children. At home they learn how to relate to others. They see how to relate to their future spouses by the way they see their mother and father relate to each other. If mom and dad argue all the time, more than likely they will grow up and argue with their spouse all the time. If dad is disrespectful to mom, the son will be disrespectful to mom and will grow up to be disrespectful to his wife. If mom does not honor her husband, neither will the daughter honor her husband. This may seem simple and common sense, but I see students all the time that do not know how to relate to other people. They are social, they know how to communicate, they know how to talk, but they do not have what we used to call common courtesies. They don't know that it is impolite to talk or interrupt someone else that is talking. They don't know how to hold a door open when someone else is coming through, just common courtesies. Where do they learn those things? AT HOME! Obviously we are failing as teachers because our children do not know how to be courteous. They do not know how to be kind and conscience of other people's feelings. And table manners are long gone.

In the world in which we live sometimes it seems that if we teach our children to be polite and show courtesy that they will be walked over and used as a doormat. This is a dog eat dog world. Every man for himself, and do whatever you have to in order to get ahead. So how does love your neighbor as thyself fit into that philosophy? It doesn't! But if it did, if we were just like the world, we would have no impact. Darkness in the dark is just dark. But shine light in the darkness and all can see. So we are to be lights in the world to shine the light of Jesus to others. Our first responsibility is to shine this light into the eyes of our own children.

We are to teach our children Godly principles and let them know that if they are saved that they have a higher calling than to live like the rest of the world. What does First John 2:15 say about the world?

"15 Love not the world, neither the things *that are* in the world. If any man love the world, the love of the Father is not in him."

____

We are not to love this world or the things of this world, but we are to lay up treasures in heaven.

John 15:20 says, "Remember the word that I said unto you, the servant is not greater than his lord. If they have persecuted me, they will also persecute you; if they have kept my saying, they will keep yours also."

Our philosophy and way of life will not be accepted by the world. They rejected Jesus so it should be no surprise when they reject us.

Even though we live in a world that is corrupt and full of evil and violence, we should still teach our children to love as Jesus loved and give as Jesus gave. This is a sacrificial type of lifestyle and one which goes against our own nature much less the worldly philosophy. But we have some promises from God to help get us through. Read Hebrews 13:5. What promise does God give us?

____

____

Read 1 John 4:1, "Ye are of God, little children, and have overcome them: because greater is he that is in you, than he that is in the world." Through Christ we are greater than anything this world can throw at us. So let us not neglect to teach our children.

To be a teacher to our child is a commandment from God with promise. What does Proverbs 22:6 say?

____

____

What are we to do?

____

What is the promise?

____

Look in the appendix at the Hebrew word for up as given in this verse. Besides train what are the other definitions of this word?

____

So when we train our children in the ways of the Lord, we are not only teaching them but we are _dedicating_ them to the ways of the Lord. A dedication is like an offering, it is our setting them apart for the Lord, so this is one way in which we can be like Hannah. We can dedicate or offer our children to the Lord by training them in His way. Read Deuteronomy 6:4-7:

"⁴ Hear, O Israel: The LORD our God is one LORD:

⁵ And thou shalt love the LORD thy God with all thine heart, and with all thy soul, and with all thy might.

⁶ And these words, which I command thee this day, shall be in thine heart:

⁷ And thou shalt teach them diligently unto thy children, and shalt talk of them when thou sittest in thine house, and when thou walkest by the way, and when thou liest down, and when thou risest up."

Who were the children of Israel supposed to teach God's words to?

____

Not only were they supposed to teach their children the words of God but God uses an adverb to describe how they were to teach them. What adverb did he use?

____

Webster's dictionary defines diligent as: characterized by steady, earnest, and energetic effort: PAINSTAKING <a *diligent* worker>

Our teaching our children God's word should be steady, not wavering. Not in church today out tomorrow. But it should be steady and constant. They should see us stick through the hard times with God and with the church and steadily keep trusting God. We should teach our children the Word of God with energetic effort. Not little effort or when I get around to it effort, but with energetic effort. It almost implies force. The Word of God should be a steady, energetic force in their lives. When and where were they supposed to teach the Words of God to their children?

____

This implies that the Word was to be taught constantly. Whatever they were doing it should be teaching their children the commandments of God. You've heard the expression, "we need to walk the talk", that is what God seems to be saying here. Yes, we are to talk to our children about it, but also walk what we talk. Live it out! If we are washing dishes, our actions should be saying, JESUS. If we are making the bed our actions should say, JESUS. If we are playing with our children, JESUS, or if we are just sitting around together, JESUS! And may our actions speak louder than our words, that we love JESUS!

Read what David says in Psalm 34:11:

"Come, ye children, hearken unto me: I will teach you the fear of the LORD."

We all know that David wears the title of "A Man After God's Own Heart", a title given him by God himself. What specifically does this man of God say he will teach the children?

____

What do the following scriptures say about "the fear of the Lord"?
    Psalm 111:10
    Proverbs 1:7
    Proverbs 9:10

____

So if we teach our children to fear the Lord we are doing them a greater service than by sending them to 12 years of school, 4 years of college, and 2 years of grad school. Wisdom is something that you cannot learn in school. True wisdom comes from realizing that God is God and he should be feared. He is an awesome and wonderful God. But He is also a terrible and all powerful God. He has the ability to raise us up and He also has the ability to cast our souls into hell. Therefore, we should have a holy, reverent fear of God. So wisdom begins here. Wisdom is much more than head knowledge. It is an inward understanding. It is insight pertaining to matters of life, and the ability to make good judgments. Let's read Proverbs 1:7-9:

"The fear of the LORD is the beginning of knowledge: but fools despise wisdom and instruction. My son, hear the instruction of thy father, and forsake not the law of thy mother: For they shall be an ornament of grace unto thy head, and chains about thy neck."
Don't you love the imagery used here:

It says that wisdom shall be ____
and instruction ____

Let's adorn our children with crowns and gold chains of royalty by teaching them to fear the Lord.

Week 6

Healer

The mother is also the healer or the caregiver. To any that have children you know that when one of them is sick or gets hurt no one else will do but Momma. From broken bones to broken hearts we do it all. We are their primary physician, orthopedic doctor, and psychiatrist all wrapped in one. I believe it is inherent, in our DNA to be caregivers. I guess that goes hand in hand with carrying them and then delivering them into this world. Before they are even born we are caring for them trying to make sure that they are well. As we carry them we are more cautious of the things we eat than ever before. We want to make sure that we eat healthy so that they eat healthy, so to speak. When they are born we take extra care to protect them and keep them healthy. Doctor visits every month to make sure they are growing as they should. And so it continues as they grow: brush your teeth, wash your face, take your medicine. Even now as a grown woman my mother is still concerned about my health and my well-being. Many times she will say, "You need to get some rest, you are doing too much". So a mother's concern for her child doesn't go away after we get them married off. I suppose that as long as we live we will care for them.

I believe this is a characteristic that we have in common with our Savior. As he walked this earth much of his time was spent healing. Anyone with an infirmity wanted to get to Jesus because he had the power to heal. But what constrained him to heal? Read the following passages and see if you can find the driving force behind his healing.

Matthew 14:14 — "And Jesus went forth, and saw a great multitude, and was moved with compassion toward them, and he healed their sick."

Matthew 20:34 — "So Jesus had compassion *on them*, and touched their eyes: and immediately their eyes received sight, and they followed him."

Mark 1:41 — "And Jesus, moved with compassion, put forth *his* hand, and touched him, and saith unto him, I will; be thou clean."

Mark 5:19 — "Howbeit Jesus suffered him not, but saith unto him, Go home to thy friends, and tell them how great things the Lord hath done for thee, and hath had compassion on thee."

Luke 7:13 — "And when the Lord saw her, he had compassion on her, and said unto her, Weep not."

So Jesus was constrained to heal by _______________________________________.

Jesus looked on them with compassion. As mothers we look on our children with compassion. If they are sick or hurting there is nothing that we would not do to make them better. This indwelling compassion to care for our children and heal them when they hurt is a Christ-like characteristic.

There are many ways in which mothers heal; these include physical, emotional, and spiritual.

I suppose when we think of healing our mind automatically goes to physical health. Part of our job as healers is to care for the physical health of our children. We try to make sure they eat right and get enough rest. We care for their boo-boos when they fall down and get scratched and cut. Band-aids® and Neosporin® are must haves for mothers of small children. And when they need more help than we can give we take them to the doctor or the hospital and we sit with them and hold their hands, ever present to be a reassuring source of strength and love.

As a healer we also care for their emotional health. We are a mighty force in this area of their lives. As we discussed earlier in the study, we can build them up or tear them down just with our words. The one place that a child should be able to go to get comfort and support is to their mom. We should be a safe haven, a place of ultimate acceptance, a place of reassurance, a place to find strength to make it through the rough times of life. Many times we cannot heal their brokenness, we can only hold them, cry with them and point them to the ONE who can. When they come to us with hurt feelings over hateful words spoken to them, we should be there to build them up. Let them know that they are special, created by God, for His purpose. And that no matter what anybody says they have worth and value in Christ. Then there are those teen years, when they start having interest in the opposite sex. And more than likely they will suffer a broken heart. I haven't had to deal with that first broken heart, but when that happens, I pray that the Lord will grant me grace and wisdom to provide the emotional strength to see my daughter through and to know that there is a brighter day. May she learn that she can always lean on me and that I love her more than life itself and that she is a precious gift from God. May I help heal her emotionally even if it's just by offering a shoulder to cry on. And may I teach my children first and foremost to find their worth in Christ. There is no man or woman that can ever fill the place in our hearts that is reserved for God alone. If they try to fill that spot with someone of the opposite sex they will never be able to have a healthy relationship of that nature. Remember the Ten Commandments; God **must** be first, above all other relationships.

Probably the most important way in which we help heal our children, and probably one of the most neglected is that of spiritual healer. We know that only God can give them spiritual healing, but we sure can help them along the way. If we instill in them a love for God, for His work, for His mission, then more than likely they will follow in that direction. We have more influence on them from the time they are born until the time when they go off on their own than anyone else. We must take advantage of this short period of time to teach our children how to be healed spiritually. The Bible says that we are a fallen race and the only way to be restored is to accept Christ as our Savior. We must constantly be pointing them to Calvary, turning their little heads to the cross. I cannot help but think of the time in the Old Testament when the snakes had come into the camp and the only way to be healed was to look upon the brazen serpent. My husband has a great message on that text by the way. Let us look at that passage from Numbers Chapter 21:

"4 And they journeyed from mount Hor by the way of the Red sea, to compass the land of Edom: and the soul of the people was much discouraged because of the way.

5 And the people spake against God, and against Moses, Wherefore have ye brought us up out of Egypt to die in the wilderness? for there is no bread, neither is there any water; and our soul loatheth this light bread.

6 And the LORD sent fiery serpents among the people, and they bit the people; and much people of Israel died.

⁷ Therefore the people came to Moses, and said, We have sinned, for we have spoken against the LORD, and against thee; pray unto the LORD, that he take away the serpents from us. And Moses prayed for the people.

⁸ And the LORD said unto Moses, Make thee a fiery serpent, and set it upon a pole: and it shall come to pass, that every one that is bitten, when he looketh upon it, shall live.

⁹ And Moses made a serpent of brass, and put it upon a pole, and it came to pass, that if a serpent had bitten any man, when he beheld the serpent of brass, he lived."

From the time of Adam until now we have all been bitten by that old serpent, sin. We were born into iniquity. We were conceived in sin. But God did not leave us hopeless. As he provided a way of escape for the children of Israel, he has also provided an escape for us. He sent his precious Son, Jesus, to hang on that old rugged cross and any that will look upon him and accept his sacrifice shall be saved. I imagine little babies and young children being bitten and how their parents must have held them up, took their hand and turned their little heads toward that brazen serpent so that their child would live. So we must do with our children. We must pick them up, turn their heads to Jesus, and help them to realize that without Him they will suffer a spiritual death that is much worse than the physical death. So mothers grab your children in your arms while they are young, hold them up, turn their little heads to Jesus that they may see, that they may see their suffering Savior and be healed.

So let us sit at the Savior's feet, take a moment to write a little prayer asking God to help you be the healer to your children that He would have you to be: one that heals physically, emotionally, and spiritually.

____

____

____

____

Week 7

Domestic Goddess/Homemaker

Cooking, cleaning, sweeping, mopping, dusting, doing laundry, these are just a few of the everyday chores of a domestic goddess. These are the things that must be done to keep a house in order and running smoothly. Traditionally these have been the duties assigned to women and even though most women are now in the work force, they still bear the biggest load of maintaining the house and doing all of the household duties. I was recently watching one of the morning shows and they had a guest on there talking about this very subject. The statistics showed that right now, in this day and age, 75% of the household chores are still done by women even though they are now working full time jobs just like their husbands. You cannot tell me that this statistic does not contribute to the high divorce rate in our society as well as in the church. When the load is so unevenly distributed frustration and resentment is bound to set in. If one person in a marriage works all day, then comes home and sits on the couch watching television all night, while the other person works all day, then comes home and works all night, there will be problems. As I said earlier in this study, I don't think God ever intended for the work-load to be so unevenly distributed. He defined our roles, but those roles have been distorted, women in our society almost have to work just to make ends meet. So since we must help our husband bear their curse, then by all means they should help us bear ours.

In many ways I think that the church contributes some of the problems that occur in marriages in our day and age. We still hear it preached that the woman should maintain the house and care for the children, which is true. But we don't hear much about men helping their working wives. So we place on women an unbearable burden. Christian women feel it is their place, their responsibility to take care of the house and if they can't or if they fall short, they feel like a failure. I know this from personal experience. Trying to work a full time job, keep up a house, and raise two children, many times I have felt like a failure, like I came short of what God designed me to do. The house and the children are my responsibility and if I don't take care of those responsibilities then I have failed. And to my own fault, I admit that I don't like for my husband to have to help me. I feel bad if he does. But I should not feel that way. We are in this thing together. We are supposed to help each other. That is why God gave us to man, to be his help-mate, not his servant; to be joint heirs with him, not his slave. So not only do we need to make men realize that if their wife is working, then they need to help her at the house. But also and maybe more difficult we need to make women realize that it is okay to ask for help from their husbands. It is okay if they have to fix a meal, change a diaper, or sweep a floor. It is okay. Remember you are helping him by working so it is okay for him to help you. There is no shame in that; it does not mean you are a failure at your God called position. It just means you are human and physically unable to carry that heavy load.

However, if a woman is fortunate enough to be able to stay home, then by all means she should take care of the house and the children. Titus 2:5 is the verse often used to define the female role:

"⁴ That they may teach the young women to be sober, to love their husbands, to love their children,

⁵ To be discreet, chaste, keepers at home, good, obedient to their own husbands, that the word of God be not blasphemed."

We pull from this verse the phrase "keepers at home". Women truly are the ones that make a house a home. I'm sure you have all heard the phrase, "if momma ain't happy, nobody's happy". In actuality that is very true. A mother truly does have a great influence over the mood of the home. So how would God have us to "keep our home"?

I believe there are two aspects to being a good homemaker. There is the physical appearance of the home and there is also the atmosphere of the home. Our tools of the trade consist of not only mops and dust clothes but also of the Bible and prayer clothes. The physical appearance of the home is important but even more essential is the spiritual atmosphere of the home. A good homemaker will not only have a clean house, but also a happy and well-balanced spiritual home.

Let us look first at the physical aspect. I believe that we should keep our homes clean and livable. It should be a place that our husband and children feel comfortable in. It should be our refuge from the world and a place of rest. As I researched the Bible looking for verses to confirm that we should keep a clean house, I could not find any that pertained specifically to keeping a clean house. But what I found over and over was verses that related to our spiritual cleanliness. That tells me, just as we talked about at the beginning of the study, God is not so concerned about the physical but He is very concerned about our spiritual well-being.

Now we will examine the spiritual aspect of being the keeper of our home. Let us take out our cleaning supplies and labor to be a good keeper of our house.

1. We must Polish Our Priorities - God Must Be First

I believe first of all to have a happy home, priorities must be in order. God clearly laid out what our priorities should be in the Ten Commandments. What was the very first commandment, see Exodus 20:3.

So God expects us to put him first. You know I have often heard it said that all problems are spiritual problems. As I think upon that statement I have come to believe that it is true. If our spiritual condition is right usually everything else will fall into place. But if we neglect to put God in His proper place then we will have problems in our spiritual life. Remember this was not a suggestion from God, but a commandment. He **must** have first place.

Since we as Christians know that there is only one true and living God, why would God say that we should have no other **gods** before him? Seems kind of strange to acknowledge something that does not exist, but looking at this verse in context of the next two verses we find that anything that we create, worship, or put before God actually becomes a god to us. Our god could be our job, our possessions, our wealth, our spouse, our children, anything that we put before God becomes our god. God, so aware of our nature and knowing how easily we can be pulled away, reminds us in the first Commandment that he must be first.

God loves us so much that He wants fellowship with us. Not just fellowship, but a spiritual intimacy that really can't be described. There is no way to reach that pinnacle unless He is first. He desires that we wake thinking of Him, that all through the day we are thinking of Him, and that when we lay our head on our pillow at night He is the last thought on our mind. He desires for our heart to long for Him. Read Deuteronomy 6:5 and fill in the blanks.

And thou shalt love the Lord thy God with all thine __________________, and with all thy _________________, and with all thy _________________.

It is so easy to put God in the back seat. To let things get ahead of Him. Especially for a woman who is wearing all of these hats and just trying to get by each day. Often we feel that we don't even have time to think much less think of God. If you are feeling this way, just take a moment now to enter the throne room and ask God to help you make time for Him. Lay your burdens at His feet, all the things you carry around and let Him help you bear the load.

2. Swept With Love

I believe that God would desire our homes to be filled with love. We should sweep away all hatred and malice and let the love of God reign in our hearts and thereby reign in our homes. Proverbs 15:17 says, "Better is a dinner of herbs where love is, than a stalled ox and hatred therewith". So God is telling us that little is much when there is love. The atmosphere of the home shapes the attitude of our children. If they are in a happy loving home, more than likely they will be happy, loving people. If they are in a home of anger and unrest, then they will more than likely grow into angry, unstable adults. Remember we are molding a generation.

So if we put God first then love will naturally follow for God is love. Read 1 John 4:7-21 and count the number of times the word love or loveth is used in this passage. Write the number in the space below.

____

God is love and he manifested his love in Jesus Christ, so we too should have that type of love. This is not a love that comes naturally because no one naturally puts others above themselves. But this is a love that comes from growing close to God and taking on his character.

It is through our love that others will know who we are. John 13:35 says, "By this shall all men know that ye are my disciples, if ye have love one to another."

How will people know that we are Christ's?

____

Taking that to a more personal level how will our family, our husbands and our children know that we are Christ's?

____

We can say all that we want to say, we can put on the perfect face for church and those we come into contact with every day, but those that live with us know the truth. It is so important that we live a life of love at home. If we are hypocrites, the first ones to see it are those that we live with, those that we are shaping. I guess it would be good to ask ourselves at this point, "Am I shaping a child of love and compassion or am I shaping a hypocrite".

We can sweep our home by loving our neighbor and by loving one another as Christ said. If we see others in need and we can help then by all means we should help. We should show the love of Christ not only to those in our own homes but to everyone. Anyone we meet or come in contact with becomes our neighbor, so our whole way of life should be one of love.

The type of love that God desires us to sweep our homes with is a self-sacrificing love. What does John 15:13 say about love?

____

So the greatest love we can show is a love of self-sacrifice. And who is our greatest example of this type of love?

____

We may never be required to actually lay down our lives to prove our love, but anytime we sacrifice our wants for the sake of others we are demonstrating that self-sacrificing type of love. And as Christ demonstrated love in the greatest degree so also He would desire us to teach that kind of love in our own homes.

3. Soaked in Forgiveness

We must soak our home in forgiveness. As Christ forgave us we are to forgive others and that should begin at home. Our families should see a woman with a forgiving spirit. When our children do wrong, and they will, if they repent we should be quick to forgive, the same way Christ forgives us. We should never hold that sin over them leaving the stain of guilt, but there should be true forgiveness that holds that thing against them no more.

Dear sister, if you are one who holds grudges and will not let things go, consider how you would feel if Christ treated you the same way. Oh, my friend, God's forgiveness is true forgiveness, complete forgiveness. When he forgives me He looks at me as though I had never sinned. He cast my sin into the sea of forgetfulness <u>never</u>, <u>never</u>, <u>never</u>, to be remembered again. Thank God, I don't have to carry the guilt because He will never throw it in my face, He remembers it no more.

There is however something that can hinder God from forgiving us. Read Matthew 6:14-15. What is it that hinders God from forgiving us?

____

So in the shadow of our Savior we are to forgive others as He forgives us. Peter asks in Matthew 18:21 "how often should we forgive a brother that sins against us". And Jesus said in verse 22 "Until seventy times seven".

What do you think he meant by that?

____

I believe He meant that as many times as someone trespasses against us, we are to forgive them. I think of Christ who had been betrayed, beaten, crowned with thorns, the beard plucked from his face, nails in his hands and feet, his side pierced through, hanging in humiliation, and as He struggled for each breath one of His last utterances from the cross was "Father forgive".

Forgiveness also is a healing agent not just for the one being forgiven, but maybe more so for the one forgiving. When we carry grudges that just makes us bitter and angry people and if we are bitter and angry we are no good to God. God desires to bless us and to use us in the kingdom work, but without a forgiving heart we are no good to God.

If you have been carrying something on your back will you not lay it down now? God desires to free you from that burden. He wants to give you deliverance and release. Also He desires for your children and those around you to see Christ in you, not bitterness. Take a moment and write a prayer to God concerning soaking your home in forgiveness.

Let us not be idle but labor to keep our houses clean, not just physically, but more importantly spiritually. May God help each of us as we try to knock down the cob webs and sweep away the dust in our spiritual home. If we can do these things we truly will be domestic goddesses.

Week 8

Accountant

Caring for the family finances is just another of the many domestic responsibilities that women have taken on in the household. A recent survey by Intuit revealed the following results:

63% of all women surveyed handle the family finances

43% of married women handle the finances alone

45% of married women share the task with their husband

11% of married women indicate no involvement

7% of all women indicate no involvement [2]

So we see that in most families the women are also the accountants or at least involved in the financial aspects of the home. Handling the finances of the home can be a very stressful responsibility. In our society it seems that most people are living beyond their means by using credit. Of course any time you use credit to buy something you become slave to the lender. God has warned us of this many times in the Word. However we still seem to go back to that same old pit. There is no wonder that finances are still amongst one of the leading causes for divorce.

So how can we balance this hat on our heads along with all of the others and keep our marriage together and create a happy home for our family? We must look to God's word for guidance in how we handle our finances. I believe that first and foremost we must realize that

---

[2] http://web:intuit.com/about-intuit/press-release/2000/05-10.html

all that we have comes from the Lord; He is the one that provides our finances. He gives us the ability to work to earn an income as well as blessing us at times in other ways.

There are three things that I believe we should consider as we look at our finances through the eyes of God. First, we must put God first in our finances. Secondly, if we are married we must realize that we are yoked together with our husbands. And thirdly, we must create some sort of budget.

1. God First In Our Finances

As with all other areas of our life, and as we talked about in the housekeeper session of our study, God must be first. It is amazing how that many people will say that they put God first yet they do not include Him in any part of their financial decisions. I believe that we can truly see a person's heart by their checkbook. If you are giving tithes and offerings to the Lord then your heart is with the Lord. If all of your money is going to fulfill material wants then your God is the material things that you are purchasing. That may seem to be a cold statement, but our God says "seek ye _first_ the kingdom of God". It is true that God does not need our money. Our God created the whole universe, but He wants us to give a portion to Him. By our giving to God, He does not get rich, but rather He accesses the condition of our heart. It is by our giving that He can truly tell if we love Him. Many people will give a few hours on Sunday, and some people will give more time to the ministry of the church, but it is a very few people that actually give their money in the way that God has told us that we should give, and that is where God measures our loyalty to Him. Read the following scripture taken from Mark 12:41-44 (NKJV):

"[41] Now Jesus sat opposite the treasury and saw how the people put money into the treasury. And many who were rich put in much.

[42] Then one poor widow came and threw in two mites, which make a quadrans.

[43] So He called His disciples to Himself and said to them, "Assuredly, I say to you that this poor widow has put in more than all those who have given to the treasury;

[44] "for they all put in out of their abundance, but she out of her poverty put in all that she had, her whole livelihood."

Where was Jesus?

____

Every time I read this passage I think of Jesus as a fly on the wall, just watching. He wasn't standing over the offering plate, but He was just quietly watching. I get the impression that those putting in money probably did not even realize He was there. Also at this point in His ministry, I don't think anyone would have given any differently just because of His presence. As Jesus watched His intent was not to see the amount of the money, but the intent of the heart.

Who did Jesus point out?

____

He did not point out those that had much to give and gave much. But He pointed out the one who had little to give, yet she gave what she had. That spoke volumes to Jesus about the condition of that woman's heart. You see Jesus is not as concerned about our money as He is about our heart.

It is with the heart that we decide what we will do with our money. It is money that runs the whole world's economies. It is a needed commodity in the world in which we live. Because of its necessity and its ability to make things happen it can easily become a God to us if we are not careful. Read 1Timothy 6:10:

"[10] For the love of money is the root of all evil: which while some coveted after, they have erred from the faith, and pierced themselves through with many sorrows."

What does Timothy say about money?

____

If you said, "it is the root of all evil" you answered incorrectly. Read the scripture again. It is not money that is the root of all evil, but rather "the love of money". Money in and of itself is neither good nor bad. But if we love money so much that it becomes our God, and we are engulfed in greed and a desire to get more and more, then money becomes an evil thing. We must be careful in our use of money and in the role it plays in our lives. We should never love it more than we love God. It should never take the place of our loving Savior who died for us.

Looking at 1 Timothy 6:10 again, how does money reward those that covet after it?

____

____

When we love money, we begin to think it is okay to stay out of church in order to earn more money. I know there are some people that have to work on Sunday and have no choice, but that is not what I am talking about. I am talking about those who don't have to, yet choose to. I am talking about those people who choose to work late just to make a little extra money rather than serving at church in whatever capacity may be needed. I am talking about those who own their own businesses, or manage companies, and can make their own schedules, yet choose to work when they could serve. I am talking about people who willingly choose making money over serving God. But I guess really they are serving their god, because whether they realize it or not, money is their god. How easy it is to err from the faith when we replace the one true and living God with an idle such as money.

Our God realizes that we need money. It truly is a necessity. We need it to buy food, clothes, & shelter. But our God still desires that we put Him first. Even above this most vital need in our lives. Read Matthew 6:31-33:

"[31] Therefore take no thought, saying, what shall we eat? Or, what shall we drink? Or, Wherewithal shall we be clothed?

[32] (For after all these things do the Gentiles seek:) for your heavenly Father knoweth that ye have need of all these things.

[33] But seek ye first the kingdom of God, and his righteousness; and all these things shall be added unto you."

What does God tell us to seek first? And what does that mean?

____

____

____

The Hebrew word used here for "seek" is "epizeteo" and it means 1) to enquire for, seek for, search for, seek diligently 2) to wish for, crave 3) to demand, clamor for. So it is more than just a glance, but it is a look in which we are searching. I imagine someone with their eyes fixed on an object, studying it intensely, trying to figure it out. So we are not just to look for God's will, but we are supposed to seek it out diligently. The things that we are to be seeking are the Kingdom of God and His righteousness.

What is the Kingdom of God?

____

____

The kingdom of God encompasses all of those that are saved; those who have accepted Jesus Christ as God's Son and have put their trust in Him. So we are to seek first to win others into the kingdom, to get people saved. That should be the first order of service in our lives as it was the first order of service in Jesus' life. Jesus said that He came to die that we may live. He says in John 12:27 that this was the very reason for Him coming to this earth:

"²⁷ Now is my soul troubled; and what shall I say? Father, save me from this hour: but for this cause came I unto this hour."

So the heart of God is to see people come to Him through Jesus Christ His Son; if we put God first then that will also be the priority of our heart. In the scope of eternity that is all that really matters. We get so caught up in the here and now that we forget about the hereafter and the importance of the choices we make or don't make for Christ. God tells us to seek *first* His kingdom.

Look at the verse again. What is the second thing that we are to seek?

____

The Bible does not say that we are to be good people, or that we are to seek after our own righteousness, for the scripture clearly states that our righteousness is as filthy rags. But rather we are to seek His righteousness.

What do you think of when you think of the righteousness of God?

The Hebrew word used here for righteousness is "dikaiosune" which means 1) in the broad sense: state of him who is as he ought to be, righteous, the condition acceptable to God 1a) the doctrine concerning the way in which man may attain a state approved of God 1b) integrity, virtue, purity of life, rightness, correctness of thinking, feeling, and acting 2) in a narrower sense, justice or the virtue which gives each his due.

To seek His righteousness is to seek true righteousness, to be in a position acceptable to God. 1 Peter 1:15-16 says,

"[15] But as he which hath called you is holy, so be ye holy in all manner of conversation;

[16] Because it is written, Be ye holy; for I am holy."

So how are we supposed to be and why?

Considering that we live in a fallen state, it almost seems as though God is asking us to do something that is impossible. And if we try to be righteous and holy in our own strength it is impossible. But it is here where we must die to self that Christ may reign in our mortal bodies. We must surrender our will to His will. As Paul said, "we struggle against the flesh", it is against our very nature to be righteous at all, much less righteous as God is righteous. However, I believe as I have heard many pastors say, the spirit battles against the flesh, but the one that we feed the most is the one that will prevail. If we feed our spirit with the word of God and stay in close communication to God through prayer and Bible reading, then our spirit will grow and God's righteousness will grow in our lives. One of my favorite scriptures and one that gives me strength when I feel week is Philippians 4:13, "I can do all things through Christ which strengtheneth me." We can't be good or righteous on our own, but with Christ we can do anything, so there is nothing impossible with God.

To get back to the point we began, God must be first in our finances, and to be first in our finances He must be first in our hearts. If we have the heart of God we will desire the things of God and it will be evident in the way we spend our money.

2. Married couples are yoked

We will serve our young people well if we instill in them this biblical view of marriage. When you marry someone you have joined yourself to that person and you are yoked together in the sight of God. This has been true since the beginning of time. Read Genesis 2:24:

"24 Therefore shall a man leave his father and his mother, and shall cleave unto his wife: and they shall be one flesh."

What does the scripture say they will be?

____

That means one vision, one direction, and financially speaking, one checkbook. When I look with both of my eyes open, I see the same thing in both eyes. When I walk, both of my legs go in the same direction. Have you ever tried to have each leg walk in a different direction? Probably not, first of all it's not natural and second, you would pull yourself apart. Now I know that is a silly analogy, but when marriage is what God intended for it to be then for the husband and wife to be going in two different directions is like trying to have your legs walk in two different directions. So when we become married we should fuse into one, become one flesh. Our vision for the future should be a shared vision. Our direction in life should be the same. And so, our checkbook should be shared. Married couples, you are in this thing together. There is no more you and me, but rather us and we.

God gives us this warning in 2 Corinthians 6:14:

"[14] Be ye not unequally yoked together with unbelievers: for what fellowship hath righteousness with unrighteousness? and what communion hath light with darkness?"

Why do you think God would give us this warning?

____

If we are not equally yoked then our desires will be different, our wants will be different, our priorities will be different, and the way we choose to spend our money will be different.

I believe that God would have us to have one checkbook. There is no longer, your money and my money. But it becomes our money. And we choose together how to spend it. Of course the bills have to be paid. But when there is extra, then a couple should choose together how they are going to spend that money. The wife might want a new pair of shoes or a new hairdo. The husband might want a new fishing rod or some new tools. So who gets what? It is up to each couple to communicate and work these kinds of things out. One person may have to submit to the other. But it is in those times that we deny ourselves that our spouses are reassured that we do love and care for them. We care enough to forgo our own wants for the sake of their wants. This should however, be a two way street. It should not be one person always submitting to the other. Otherwise resentment will build up and destroy the relationship. I am reminded of that old story where the man sold his watch to buy his wife a barrette for her long beautiful hair. While unknowingly she cut and sold her hair to buy him a chain for his watch. And the moral of the story was that they both loved each other so much that they were willing to give up something valuable to them in order to get something nice for the other. Also a little submission builds character, and as I have said before, we are most like our Savior when we submit ourselves to one another.

So when it comes to our finances we need to remember that we are yoked together. We share everything, even the checkbook. I guess I should say especially the checkbook since that is the engine that keeps things running financially.

3. Must Create a Budget

If you are to wear the hat of accountant and be successful at it then you must prepare some sort of a budget. A budget is a means of control. If you have no budget then you have no control over your money and if you don't watch your money before you know it, it will be gone and you will not know where it went. My dad used to tell me if you watch your pennies and nickels your dollars will take care of themselves. That means if we are careful down to the least amount we will not have to worry about where our money goes. Read Luke 14:28-30:

"28 For which of you, intending to build a tower, sitteth not down first, and counteth the cost, whether he have sufficient to finish it?

29 Lest haply, after he hath laid the foundation, and is not able to finish it, all that behold it begin to mock him,

30 Saying, This man began to build, and was not able to finish."

What is God telling us through this scripture?

____

If we start without a plan we are likely to end in disaster. In my 20 years of marriage I have tried it both ways and believe me it always works better when you have a budget. A good budget will look at income, expenses, and what is left over. But one of the foremost things to consider and one of the things that many people leave out is tithes. God says that we are to give Him our first fruits so that should be the first thing we consider. Also I put a place for savings above the other expenses. I have taught Personal Finance using the Dave Ramsey curriculum for several years and this is what he suggested, and I agree with him. He says you have to "pay yourself first." There are a variety of ways you can save. You can save through a savings account or retirement plans such as a 401K through your employer or an IRA. If you don't make savings a priority, there is no doubt, you will spend the money. I can speak from personal experience. Below I have an example of a basic budget. Now you may have to adjust this budget to your own personal needs, but it is an example of some of the things you need to account for when preparing your budget.

BUDGET

Income ___________

    Tithes ___________

    Taxes ___________

    Savings ___________

Net Income ___________

Fixed Expenses

    Mortgage/Rent ___________

    Car Payment ___________

    Car Insurance ___________

    Health Insurance ___________

Unfixed Expenses

    Food/Groceries ___________

    Utilities ___________

    Cable/Satellite ___________

    Telephone ___________

    Gasoline & oil ___________

    Parking & tolls ___________

    Repairs ___________

    Cell Phone ___________

    Medical Expenses ___________

    Clothing ___________

    Entertainment ___________

    Household Items ___________

    Hair Cuts ___________

    School Expenses ___________

Total Expenses ___________

Net Income – Expenses ___________

One important thing to remember when preparing a budget is that the budget is the financial plan for the home; therefore both the husband and wife should take part in preparing it. It directs where your money goes and what you can and cannot spend. If both parties are not in agreement about the budget then there will be problems.

I must come to this point again; we must give back to God *first*. As I said previously, where we put our money speaks volumes to the condition of our heart in relation to God. So as we balance this hat on our heads let us consider God first, that we are yoked, and that to be successful in our finances we need to develop a budget to live by.

Week 9

Philanthropist/Charity Worker/Volunteer

Amidst all of their other duties many women still find time to wear this hat. This is not a hat that we must wear but for whatever reason many times we get drawn into these types of service. Philanthropy is defined as goodwill to fellowmen; active effort to promote human welfare. The Philanthropist is a person that tries to support and raise money for a good cause. Many women get catapulted into this type of service by circumstances that affect them directly. I have heard of many women that through a disease or illness in their own family they have become involved in raising money and trying to find a cure for that particular disease or illness.

We also have many charity workers amongst us who work in soup kitchens and health clinics. They dedicate their time, effort, and skill to try to help others that are maybe less fortunate. Many women show charity and don't even realize it. When you give a person in need something to eat, when you help a neighbor or a friend pay a utility bill so they won't get their electricity turned off. Even when you reach out to someone in love just to encourage them, maybe with a card or just a pat on the back, you are showing charity. What does charity really mean?

The word "charity" especially used in the Bible means "love". When we show charity we are actually showing love. Love to others. And I am sure that at some point in our lives we have all been drawn into the role of volunteer. How many times have mothers volunteered to help in their children's schools, or volunteered to help coach a ball team, lead a Girl Scout squad, or a Boy Scout's troop?

It is in this role that we reach out beyond our own families and show the love of Christ to others. It is normal to love and care for our own families; but when we go beyond that and love those outside our circle, that is when we are fulfilling the commandment that Jesus gave us, "love thy neighbor as thyself". Read Matthew 22:35- 40.

"[35] Then one of them, which was a lawyer, asked him a question, tempting him, and saying,

[36] Master, which is the great commandment in the law?

[37] Jesus said unto him, Thou shalt love the Lord thy God with all thy heart, and with all thy soul, and with all thy mind.

[38] This is the first and great commandment.

[39] And the second is like unto it, Thou shalt love thy neighbor as thyself.

[40] On these two commandments hang all the law and the prophets."

What is the great commandment?

____

What is the second greatest commandment?

____

All of the law and prophets hang on these two commandments. So it does not matter if we are good people and we don't lie, steal, kill, commit adultery, etc. if we do not first love our God and then love others. It is the love of God that reigns in us that shows the world that we are His. And it is that love that compels us to love others, to have compassion on others as Christ has had compassion on us.

I love the story of the Good Samaritan. It teaches us to look beyond our prejudice, beyond our time constraints, beyond ourselves to the needs of others. Read the story of the Good Samaritan in Luke 10:29-37.

"²⁹ But he, willing to justify himself, said unto Jesus, And who is my neighbor?

³⁰ And Jesus answering said, A certain man went down from Jerusalem to Jericho, and fell among thieves, which stripped him of his raiment, and wounded him, and departed, leaving him half dead.

³¹ And by chance there came down a certain priest that way: and when he saw him, he passed by on the other side.

³² And likewise a Levite, when he was at the place, came and looked on him, and passed by on the other side.

³³ But a certain Samaritan, as he journeyed, came where he was: and when he saw him, he had compassion on him,

³⁴ And went to him, and bound up his wounds, pouring in oil and wine, and set him on his own beast, and brought him to an inn, and took care of him.

³⁵ And on the morrow when he departed, he took out two pence, and gave them to the host, and said unto him, Take care of him; and whatsoever thou spendest more, when I come again, I will repay thee.

³⁶ Which now of these three, thinkest thou, was neighbor unto him that fell among the thieves?

³⁷ And he said, He that shewed mercy on him. Then said Jesus unto him, Go, and do thou likewise."

Here we have this smart aleck lawyer trying to trip Jesus up by asking him "who is my neighbor." Our neighbor is anyone that we see in need. It is our responsibility to reach out to those in need and show them the love of Jesus. To show them mercy as Jesus showed us mercy.

If you remember when we started this study we looked at the woman of Proverbs 31, read again verse 20:

"

²⁰ She stretcheth out her hand to the poor; yea, she reacheth forth her hands to the needy."
Right in the midst of all her duties and all that she does for her family we find this verse.

What is she doing in this verse?

____

Notice the verbs, in the KJV what verbs are used?

____

She stretches out and reaches forth beyond her own circle, her own family, to her neighbor. I image one reaching and stretching the arm, stretching to the place that the whole body is leaning in that direction, pulled out of position, to the point of being uncomfortable even, stretching out to be a help and a blessing to others.

So ladies when you get tired and you think why in the world am I doing this, just remember you are stretching. You are reaching forth with the love of Jesus to help others; others who may not have been quite as fortunate as you, those who maybe are having a hard time, those who may be down on their luck. Those who need a stretched out hand to help pull them up out of the pit that they are in. Don't stop reaching forth and stretching out with the love of Jesus, but rather reach a little farther, stretch until your muscles feel like they are going to snap like a rubber band. And may the world know that our Jesus is alive and that His love is real and that He is the answer to all of life's questions and all of life's problems for He is ALL in ALL. Thank you Jesus!

Week 10

Physical Appearance/Beauty Queen

You may be wondering why I would list physical appearance as a hat that a woman wears. Well mainly because it is a big part of our lives. We are bombarded with images of beautiful people, especially beautiful women. All forms of media from magazines to television project the image of the beautiful and the perfect woman. We see these images and we want to be beautiful too. Don't be super spiritual and tell me that appearance doesn't matter to you, because my question will be, "how much money do you spend on make-up, clothes, and hair styling products." We feel a need, whether consciously or subconsciously, to be beautiful.

Many of us as older women have come to accept what we were given at birth and to work with it the best we can. However, our teen age girls are also being bombarded with images of the beautiful and many of them feel inferior because they feel that they don't stack up to what a young girl should be. They may not realize that what they are looking at is not real either, but it has been air brushed, digitally touched-up, etc. to make it appear as a beautiful image. Or it could be that the person in the photograph has actually had cosmetic surgery to improve her appearance.

It was from this very epidemic that Dove launched its "Campaign for Real Beauty." This campaign was to open up discussion about what real beauty is and to employ real women to be models for their products.[3] When a major company such as Dove sees a problem with how we portray beauty, then you know there is a real crisis.

---

[3] http://www.dove.us/#/CFRB/arti_cfrb.aspx[cp-documentid=7049726]/

We have become so vain that we are rushing to go under the knife to improve our appearance. There were over 14.6 million cosmetic plastic surgery procedures in 2012 which was an increase of 5% over 2011.[4]

Let's look at the following information provided by the American Society of Plastic Surgeons. The top five surgical cosmetic procedures in 2012 were: 1) Breast Augmentation with a total of 286, 274 women having this procedure done. 2) Nose Reshaping with a total number of 242,684 people having this procedure. Of that number 180,913 were female and 61,771 were male. 3) Liposuction with a total of 202,128 people having this procedure. Of that number 179,214 were female and 22,914 were male. 4) Eyelid surgery with a total of 204,015 people having this procedure, 174,965 were female and 29,050 were male. 5) Tummy Tuck had a total of 106,628 having this procedure, 102,277 were female and 4,351 were male.

The top five minimally-invasive cosmetic procedures in 2012 were as follows: 1) Botox® with a total of 6,134,621 people having this procedure. Of that number 5,745,052 were female and 389,569 were male. 2) Chemical peel had a total of 1,133,821 having this procedure. Of that number 1,043,405 were female and 90,416 were male. 3) Laser hair removal with a total of 1,118,254 having this procedure, 924,317 were female and 193,937 were male. 4) Microdermabrasion with a total of 973,556 people having this procedure, 790,902 were female and 182,654 were male. 5) Hyaluronic acid with a total of 1,423,136 having this procedure, 1,381,227 were female and 41,909 were male.

Now keep in mind, these procedures are purely cosmetic, which means they are not for any health reasons. Also this means that insurance companies will not pay for these procedures. The people having these procedures have such image issues that they are willing to pay out of their pocket or go in debt to have these procedures done. When you look at these numbers and consider what is happening in our culture it is staggering that we have become so vain and so image driven in our society. From "Extreme Makeover" to "The Swan" to the Discovery Health's "Plastic Surgery: Before and After" we find people desperate to change the way they look. I remember watching one of those shows and the person having surgery was so obsessed with her looks. I thought how sad. How sad to be so consumed by something that is going to grow old and wrinkle up and die. No matter how much cosmetic surgery one has it is inevitable, we all grow old and die. The real thing that we should be worried about is the condition

---

[4] http://www.plasticsurgery.org/Documents/news-resources/statistics/2012-Plastic-Surgery-Statistics/Cosmetic-Procedure-Trends-2012.pdf

of our soul. It is a sad state when we are more concerned about our outward appearance than our eternal soul.

Now don't get me wrong, I still believe in the old saying, "a little caulk, a little paint, will make it what it ain't". And I know ain't ain't a word. I like to have my hair done, wear nice clothes, and put some make-up on. I like to look the best I can (most of the time). But we cannot get to the point to believe that the outward appearance is the most important thing. I am afraid that is where we are in our society. That is the message that is being sent throughout the media. But my question is, "What does God say about physical appearance?" Read 1 Samuel 16:7:

"But the LORD said to Samuel, "Do not look at his appearance or at the height of his stature, because I have refused him. For *the LORD does* not *see* as man sees; for man looks at the outward appearance, but the LORD looks at the heart."

What does man look at?

____

What does God look at?

____

Does this not sound familiar? Throughout much of the study we have said that God is concerned with the condition of our hearts. And so it is clearly stated here. He doesn't care if we are pretty, tall, long-legged, blonde hair, blue eyes. Thank you Jesus! If God looked only at the physical appearance I would be left out. But you see He looks much deeper, He looks to our heart, our character, to who we really are. You know one of these days those of us who have accepted Christ are going to receive an "Extreme Makeover", we are going to drop this old flesh like an old garment and the Lord is going to give us a perfect, glorified body. What a day that will be! But for now why worry so much about that old garment, rather take care of the thing that is eternal, the spirit that resides inside of this mortal flesh.

When our appearance becomes too important to us, when it becomes our main focus, then we become vain. To be vain, according to Webster's Dictionary, is having or showing undue or excessive pride in one's appearance or achievements. And why do we need to worry about our spiritual condition when we become so vain?

I believe it is about focus. If we are a vain person where is our focus?

____

Our focus is probably on ourselves. And where should our focus be?

____

Remember anything that takes priority over God is an idol. So when we become vain we teeter on breaking one of the Ten Commandments and committing idolatry. Imagine that, we can make our own selves into an idol, now how vain can one be, to take God off of the throne and take residence there as if we deserved that position. Let's consider the first person that tried that. Read Isaiah 14:12-14

"12 How art thou fallen from heaven, O Lucifer, son of the morning! How art thou cut down to the ground, which didst weaken the nations!

13 For thou hast said in thine heart, I will ascend into heaven, I will exalt my throne above the stars of God: I will sit also upon the mount of the congregation, in the sides of the north:

14 I will ascend above the heights of the clouds; I will be like the most High."

Who is this scripture talking about?

____

Satan himself introduced vanity into the universe. Read that scripture again and count the number of I's you find.

If I counted correctly 5 times Satan declares what he will do. That is why this Cherub was cast out of heaven. That is why he is our foe even to this day. So when we become vain, our focus moves from God to I and we become like Satan.

So let us refocus! Let us take the focus off of ourselves and put it back on God. Let us not be so concerned about our outward appearance, but rather about the appearance of our heart. If God looks at the heart of man, what does He see when He looks at you? No let me make that more personal, what does He see when He looks at me?

Week 11

Church Worker

This title encompasses anyone who does anything in the local church, whether it be teaching Sunday School, cooking Wednesday night meals, working in the children's ministry, singing in the choir or any other type of service you perform in the church. If you are going through this study then more than likely you are a church worker or you will be a church worker. Why do I say this? Because those that are interested in trying to improve themselves spiritually will probably also be the ones that are serving. For it is a person like you that truly loves the Lord and wants to serve Him and wants to become more like Him.

This is the last role that we cover but it certainly is not the least. This role, much like that of the charity worker, involves our voluntary service. It is not like the hat of mother where, once you become a mother, there is no backing out. That baby is yours to raise and you have the responsibility. You can't say, "Well I don't think I want to be a mother today". But as a church worker you can choose to serve or not to serve. If you want to take a day off you have that prerogative. That is why this role is so special. Because you exercise your free will to serve or not to serve your Lord. And let's be honest if it were not for the women serving in the church, it could not function.

To serve we must become humble

If we want an example of the greatest servant to the church we need look no further than to the cross. Our Savior was the ultimate church worker. All the work He did was for the church. From the first breath He took in that stable in Bethlehem until His last breath on Calvary, our

Jesus was working for *us*, His church. Throughout his life he showed us His servant spirit. He humbled himself that He may serve us.

He humbled himself when He left his home in glory, came to this wicked world, and died on a cruel cross, just for us. Read Philippians 2:7-8:

"⁷ But made himself of no reputation, and took upon him the form of a servant, and was made in the likeness of men:

⁸ And being found in fashion as a man, he humbled himself, and became obedient unto death, even the death of the cross".

According to Philippians 2:7 what three things did He do when he came to this earth?

____

____

____

And after He was fashioned as a man, according to verse 8, what did He do?

____

His mere act of coming to this earth showed humility, but He went even further. Here we find that the Creator humbled Himself before His own creation. He was not worried about His reputation, that He may not be recognized as the Son of God. This takes some humility. To humble oneself at all is hard for this old flesh, but to humble yourself to the one you created; to have the power to give life or death, and yet to humble yourself. Also notice that He did not do this in His glorified state, but as a man, a flesh and blood man. He took on the same flesh that we live in and he had control over it to the point to humble himself, as the Bible says even to the death of the cross. So He asks us to do nothing that He has not done Himself.

In John chapter 13 we again find our savior serving. He is serving this time in one of the most humbling ways. Here we see our Savior girding himself with a towel, taking a basin of water and going one by one to each disciple and washing their feet. This was a job that the lowliest of servants would do. And here is Jesus the Savior of the World, the Son of God, The Prince of Peace, The Lily of the Valley, The Bright and Morning Star, here He is washing the feet of these rugged men. Now keep in mind, these were rugged men. Not like some of these metro-sexual men that we have today that would have a perfectly pedicured foot. These men probably walked everywhere they went in sandaled feet so there feet would have been dirty and possibly bruised and cut. And our lovely Savior bows down on his knees takes the foot of each man, takes a towel in his lovely hands, and washes these dirty, filthy, rugged feet. WHAT HUMILITY!

As I read this passage I think when was the last time I bowed on my knees for someone else? Not to wash their feet, but to lift them up in prayer. To help wash my brother or sister who is struggling with the water of my tears and my prayers. This is also a humbling experience because it takes time and we must put someone else before ourselves. As church workers this is one area that we could really find a true ministry work – praying for others. My challenge to you is to get someone on your heart and pray for them and their situation on a daily basis.

Write below the name of the person that you will humble yourself before God to intercede for.

____

Read John 13:14-15, this is what Jesus said to His disciples after He had washed their feet. "If I then, your Lord and Master, have washed your feet; ye also ought to wash one another's feet. For I have given you an example, that ye should do as I have done to you."

According to this scripture, why did Jesus wash the disciples' feet?

____

Our service is voluntary

And all of this Christ did voluntarily. He came to earth voluntarily. His life's ministry was voluntary. His washing of the disciples' feet was voluntary. And His death on the cross was voluntary. Read John 10:17-18:

"[17] Therefore doth my Father love me, because I lay down my life, that I might take it again.

[18] No man taketh it from me, but I lay it down of myself. I have power to lay it down, and I have power to take it again. This commandment have I received of my Father."
What does this scripture say about Christ's death?

____

It was voluntary. No man took it from him, but rather He freely laid it down; so sister our voluntary service that we do for the church is no small thing. It reflects the heart of Christ when we voluntarily work for Him.

We often think of the high and the mighty as being great in God's kingdom but that is not necessarily so. God loves a volunteer spirit. He loves a spirit that will give to others and serve for others. Read Mark 10:43-45:

"But so shall it not be among you: but whosoever will be great among you, shall be your minister:

And whosoever of you will be the chiefest, shall be servant of all.

For even the Son of man came not to be ministered unto, but to minister, and to give his life a ransom for many."

To be great in the kingdom of God we must ____________________________________.
To be chief we must ____.

The person with a servant's heart is the person with God's heart. God as we have said before does not look at the outward appearance of man or the outward show of man, but rather God looks at the heart of man. What is the purpose for what we do? Do we do it because we love the Lord or because we seek status? If you are working in the church then more than likely you are not doing it for status or recognition but because you love your Lord.

How do we serve?

You may ask "How can I serve"? There are many ways you can serve and normally the Lord will lead you where He has a plan and purpose for you, _if_ you will follow him. It is clear from scripture that He expects us to use our talents and our gifts for His service. Remember the parable in the Bible about the master who left his servants talents and when he came back two had earned more talents but the one had hid his talent in the ground. The master was not happy with this servant because he had hid his talent instead of using it. God expects us to use our talents.

We all do not have great talents but if we have been saved God has given us gifts and He expects us to use them. Remember the lady in the Bible that anointed Jesus' head? Let's read that scripture from Mark 14: 1-8:

"After two days was the feast of the Passover, and of unleavened bread: and the chief priests and the scribes sought how they might take him by craft, and put him to death.

But they said, Not on the feast day, lest there be an uproar of the people.

And being in Bethany in the house of Simon the leper, as he sat at meat, there came a woman having an alabaster box of ointment of spikenard very precious; and she brake the box, and poured it on his head.

And there were some that had indignation within themselves, and said, Why was this waste of the ointment made?

For it might have been sold for more than three hundred pence, and have been given to the poor. And they murmured against her.

And Jesus said, Let her alone; why trouble ye her? She hath wrought a good work on me.

For ye have the poor with you always, and whensoever ye will ye may do them good: but me ye have not always.

She hath done what she could: she is come aforehand to anoint my body to the burying."

What did this lady do?

____

How did the some of the people around react to this ladies action?

____

____

There will always be naysayers, but you can't let that get you down. You just keep on serving the Lord. You may feel led to do something in the church or start a new ministry and there will be those that will say "we can't do that". You just respond, "we can't but God can" and keep serving the Lord. You are not doing it for those around you anyways but rather for the glory of the Lord.

How did Jesus respond to her actions?

____

He approved! He even defended her and told them to leave her alone. Our God is capable of stopping the mouths of those that would cast criticism on our service and on our worship.

I think the phrase that catches my attention the most in this passage is when Jesus says, "She hath done what she could". This was a very expensive ointment that she poured upon his head. Nevertheless all she did was pour it. There was no great act, no great words, no wondrous miracles, just a woman pouring ointment on the Saviors head. And yet it pleased the Lord. Jesus implies that somehow the woman realized that Jesus would soon die. And so this ointment served to prepare his body for burying. This was an act of love, praise, and worship.

Our God does not ask us to do anything beyond our means, He just expects us to do what we can. And we can do much if we are surrendered to God. What does Philippians 4:13 say that we can do?

I can do all things through Christ which strengtheneth me.

What can we do?

____

How can we do it?

____

If God has called us to serve in His church there is nothing we cannot do. He will empower us to be successful and to be fruitful in the work of the kingdom of God.

Why should we labor?

We should labor for the glory of the Lord; that others may see Him magnified in our lives. Read 1 Peter 4:11:

"If any man speak, let him speak as the oracles of God; if any man minister, let him do it as of the ability which God giveth: that God in all things may be glorified through Jesus Christ, to whom be praise and dominion for ever and ever. Amen."

If we speak we should speak _________________________________.
If we minister we should do it as of ______________________________.
That God in all things may be __________________________________.

Our God is worthy of all praise and glory and honor and when we serve him in our speech and in our walk it brings glory to His Holy name. So may we be vigilant about what we say and what we do and how we live that we may never bring shame but always bring glory to the God of heaven.

Dear sister there may be times when you get discouraged and down hearted, there may be times when you wonder, "why am I doing this" and "what difference does it make". We can find comfort in 1 Corinthians 15:58:

"Therefore, my beloved brethren, be ye stedfast, unmoveable, always abounding in the work of the Lord, forasmuch as ye know that your labour is not in vain in the Lord."

What does the word say about our labor?

____

Our God will reward us for our labor; it is not in vain. One day in heaven we will receive a reward for serving him. Also we will get to see others that we led to Christ or maybe those that we taught in Sunday school or one that we served a meal to. To see people that we ministered to in heaven will be reward in itself.

Who do we labor with?

We can find comfort, strength, and support in 1 Corinthians 3:9:

"For we are laborers together with God: ye are God's husbandry, ye are God's building."

There is great comfort and reassurance in this verse because it reaffirms the fact that we are not alone.

Who do we labor with?

____

How glorious to know that I am not alone. Not only that, but it is God that is with me if God be for me then who can stand against me. I am laboring with the greatest of the greats, the King of Kings, and the Lord of Lords. I AM NOT ALONE! Thank you Jesus. You do not just send us into the battle, but you go with us. And I know that you will give us victory.

So as we try to juggle this last hat, let us not lose sight of the importance of this hat. Yes it is a hat that we could easily sling to the side. But consider what would be left undone if we did not work in God's church to increase His Kingdom.

Week 12

Conclusion

So in conclusion I hope that you have found encouragement for the busy life that you are living. I know that I have not given you any kind of miraculous formula to make it easier. But I hope that you have come to realize as I have, that it is not so much about the hat that we wear as it is about how we wear it. My role as wife is shallow if I do not reflect Christ to my husband as I wear that hat. The same is true with my role as a mother, a worker, or any other hat that I wear. If others see me in those roles but they don't see Jesus then I have failed. There may be dishes in the sink and toys from one end of the house to the other, but does that really matter in light of eternity. If I am yelling and complaining and all my children see is a grumpy old woman, then I have failed. I have let life get the best of me and I have stopped living: I have forgotten the most needful thing. I must put down the dish towel and sit at the Savior's feet for it is there that I will find my strength.

I have come to realize that my plate is full. Yes, completely full and I cannot do it all. Believe it or not, I have realized that I AM NOT SUPERWOMAN! But you know what, God already knows that and furthermore, He doesn't expect me to be. Another thing I have learned as I juggle these hats and try to keep them all in the air is that yes, my plate is full, but in reality it is not my plate. It is God's plate. I am just an instrument in his hand. I need to stop trying to own it all and hand it over to Him. For my God is capable of handling it.

Even though we know that God is in control life is still difficult at times. I can relate to much of what you as a woman goes through because I go through it too. In the morning when I have to pull myself from my baby girl who is clinging with all her might, her little arms clasped around my neck saying, 'Mommy don't go", I know what that is like. I know what it is like driving to work, with your eyes glassed over as you try to hold back the tears. Then tears welling up to overflowing and running down your face streaking up your makeup. I know what that is like. I know what it is like to see your oldest child start driving and wondering, "Where did my baby go". I know what it is like to be so tired because you were up the night before with a baby or a sick child and thinking how am I going to have the strength to get through the day. But I have found that it is in those times when I am weak and when I am vulnerable that I am driven to sit at the feet of Jesus. And when I arise I am refreshed and renewed. For my Jesus gives me strength, He comforts me; he is my all and all. In Him and only in Him can I ever be the mother, wife, worker/provider, homemaker, healer, teacher, accountant, beauty queen, charity worker, and church worker that I ought to be. ONLY IN HIM!

And so we come full circle in our study and we find that to do any of these things with any amount of success we must first sit at the feet of Jesus. Sometimes we need to have a Mary attitude and not always be like Martha. Don't neglect the most needful thing. STOP! Slow down and take time to learn of Him. If we don't learn of Him how will we know how to wear these hats and fulfill these roles? He is the one who teaches and instructs us in life. He would not have us be cumbered, but rather He desires that we be refreshed and energized to wear our hats high; that we may bring glory to our Savior in all the roles of life.

We should strive to be a Proverbs 31 woman. Remember her from the beginning or our study? She was such an exemplary woman that she received almost an entire chapter in the book of wisdom. Before we conclude this study let us read her testimony one more time and find encouragement to carry on the torch.

Proverbs 31:10-31

"10 Who can find a virtuous woman? for her price is far above rubies.

11 The heart of her husband doth safely trust in her, so that he shall have no need of spoil.

12 She will do him good and not evil all the days of her life.

"13 She seeketh wool, and flax, and worketh willingly with her hands.

14 She is like the merchants' ships; she bringeth her food from afar.

15 She riseth also while it is yet night, and giveth meat to her household, and a portion to her maidens.

¹⁶ She considereth a field, and buyeth it: with the fruit of her hands she planteth a vineyard.

¹⁷ She girdeth her loins with strength, and strengtheneth her arms.

¹⁸ She perceiveth that her merchandise is good: her candle goeth not out by night.

¹⁹ She layeth her hands to the spindle, and her hands hold the distaff.

²⁰ She stretcheth out her hand to the poor; yea, she reacheth forth her hands to the needy.

²¹ She is not afraid of the snow for her household: for all her household are clothed with scarlet.

²² She maketh herself coverings of tapestry; her clothing is silk and purple.

²³ Her husband is known in the gates, when he sitteth among the elders of the land.

²⁴ She maketh fine linen, and selleth it; and delivereth girdles unto the merchant.

²⁵ Strength and honour are her clothing; and she shall rejoice in time to come.

²⁶ She openeth her mouth with wisdom; and in her tongue is the law of kindness.

²⁷ She looketh well to the ways of her household, and eateth not the bread of idleness.

²⁸ Her children arise up, and call her blessed; her husband also, and he praiseth her.

²⁹ Many daughters have done virtuously, but thou excellest them all.

³⁰ Favour is deceitful, and beauty is vain: but a woman that feareth the LORD, she shall be praised.

³¹ Give her of the fruit of her hands; and let her own works praise her in the gates."

You may wonder how she could be so good. I think the answer is found in verse 30. What does the verse say?

____

____

Our ability to be a great woman, the kind of woman that will bring honor to our husbands and children, and our God stems from a genuine fear of the Lord. Read Psalm 111:10:

"The fear of the LORD is the beginning of wisdom: a good understanding have all they that do his commandments: his praise endureth forever."

What does Psalm 111:10 say about fear?

____

It is where we begin. If we fear Him we will bow before Him. If we make time for Him in our busy schedule, he will make time for us. He will make our time more productive. We won't struggle around and back track and get off course, but He will make things flow and order will come to our chaotic existence. He will make it where we are not just struggling through life but enjoying the journey; enjoying those moments with our husband when we can laugh and be happy just to be together. He will let us enjoy our children and savor every moment, knowing that time goes so quickly and before you know it they will have their own lives. He will let us enjoy even the housekeeping. Even those dirty dishes can be a joy when we are washing them for the glory of the Lord. He can make our charity work and our church work a joy and not a grudge. We can reflect Christ to those in need or those we are ministering to. We can enjoy those times of healing and teaching. We can enjoy even those times when it seems like we can't make ends meet financially. Even then we can enjoy life knowing that His ends always meet and He is fully able to provide all our needs. But it is only in Him, only in Jesus that we can enjoy the journey.

So dear ladies as you try to topple those hats on your head, they reach no higher than when you bow your head and kneel at the feet of Jesus. Give Him your hats; give Him all the roles of life. Can't you just see those hats standing straight, reaching tall, as you sit at his feet? Do they not become lighter, as if a weight was lifted in the presence of our Lord? Lay it at His feet and He will give you strength to wear those hats with honor and in a way that brings glory and honor to His holy, precious name. And remember that the most needful thing is to take time to sit at the feet of Jesus!

Appendix

Help Meet

> Hebrew Word: ezer
> Meaning: to help, succor

Woman

> Hebrew Word: ishshah
> Meaning: woman, wife, female

Cleave

> Hebrew Word: dabaq
> Meaning: to cling, stick, stay close, cleave, keep close, stick to, stick with, follow closely, join to, overtake, catch

Sorrow

> Hebrew Word: itstsabown
> Meaning: pain, labor, hardship, sorrow, toil

Desire

> Hebrew Word: tĕshuwqah
> Meaning: desire, longing, craving

Scriptures establishing God's order

Ephesians 5:22-24 - Wives, submit yourselves unto your own husbands, as unto the Lord. For the husband is the head of the wife, even as Christ is the head of the church: and he is the saviour of the body. Therefore as the church is subject unto Christ, so [let] the wives [be] to their own husbands in every thing.

Hebrews 13:17 - Obey them that have the rule over you, and submit yourselves: for they watch for your souls, as they that must give account, that they may do it with joy, and not with grief: for that [is] unprofitable for you.

1 Peter 2:13-19 - Submit yourselves to every ordinance of man for the Lord's sake: whether it be to the king, as supreme; Or unto governors, as unto them that are sent by him for the punishment of evildoers, and for the praise of them that do well. For so is the will of God, that with well doing ye may put to silence the ignorance of foolish men: As free, and not using [your] liberty for a cloke of maliciousness, but as the servants of God. Honour all [men]. Love the brotherhood. Fear God. Honour the king. Servants, be subject to your masters with all fear; not only to the good and gentle, but also to the froward. For this is thankworthy, if a man for conscience toward God endure grief, suffering wrongfully.

Enmity

Hebrew Word: eybah
Meaning: enmity, hatred

Advocate

Meaning: one that pleads the cause of another

Comfort

Hebrew Word: nacham
Meaning: to be sorry, console oneself, repent, regret, comfort, be comforted

Up

Hebrew Word: chanak
Meaning: to train, dedicate, inaugurate